NOTHING STOOD IN HER WAY,

Captain Julie Clark

with Ann Lewis Cooper

ISBN: 1-4782-8200-2
ISBN-13: 9781478282006

Cover photo by Chris Nelson
Post processing by Marilyn Kendrick

CONTENTS

A Foreword
by Dr. Peggy Chabrian
Founder and President,
Women in Aviation, International

My first encounter with Julie Clark was from a distance, looking up in the sky, watching her perform an aerobatic routine at an air show. Two things struck me during her routine – her patriotism as evidenced by the music she selected to be played while she performed her aerobatics as well as the grace of flying her T-34.

It was a few years later that I had the opportunity to meet her in person and to learn she had a second aviation career, captain for Northwest Airlines. In this first personal encounter, I was impressed with her professionalism and enthusiasm, for aviation and for life.

In the pages of this book you will come to know Julie Clark, from personal tragedies that struck her family when she was very young to her successes as both an airshow and airline pilot. And on the way, learn of her determination to succeed, to try new ventures, and to recover from setbacks.

Julie's story will entertain both the aviation professional and enthusiast as well as a reader interested in a biography of a fascinating life.

A Dedication

With a Special Thanks
to "Mac",
whose patience is rock solid,
~and who always has had my back.
No matter what!
I dedicate my biography
to the memory of my parents,
Marge and Ernie Clark.
They gave me the base upon which
I've built my life. Their Inspiration and
Love have sustained me. They have
been with me in spirit during every hour
and every mile that I've flown.

I further dedicate this to my sisters,
Judy Grilli and Sharon De Vos.
My love and thanks to them.
I can't imagine what
life would have been like
without them.

Captain Julie Clark boards for flight

On the flightline, Northwest Airlines

Photos by David Poleski

NOTHING STOOD IN HER WAY,
Captain Julie Clark

with Ann Lewis Cooper

CHAPTER ONE: ADMIRERS GATHER

On the evening of 15 October 2003, a California ranch house on Boeing Road in Cameron Park, high in the foothills above the Sacramento Valley, held its breath, waiting for an important and gala event. Preparations had taken the better part of two months. The home glowed more elegantly and invitingly than any Kincaid painting could hope to do, its lighting creating a holiday ambiance and warmth. The yard twinkled with lights decorating the branches of the backyard foliage and the home pulsated with music, its front door opening wide like welcoming arms reaching for invited guests, urging them to join the festivities.

As the party hour neared, savory odors of warm hors d'oeuvres mingled with the crisp smells of autumn and boisterous, happy guests tumbled out of their cars – or airplanes – to surround the home's owner, Julie Clark. Reveling in having reached an apex in one career, Julie was celebrating retirement from Northwest Airlines. Her magical night crowned the success of an admirable thirty-five years in the airline industry, twenty-seven years as an airline pilot, and twenty years as a captain. Here she was surrounded affectionately by many of her fans and friends. Although no gifts had been requested of those invited to the party, one long table

Julie Clark graces the captain's seat for her final flight with Northwest Airlines, 9 October 2003

held the cards and gifts attesting to the loving outpouring of those who could not attend the auspicious event.

An adjacent hangar, normally housing two meticulously maintained military trainers – a Beech T-34A *Mentor* and a North American T-28C *Trojan* – had been emptied to accommodate the revelers. The T-34 and T-28 had been moved for the evening, but the hangar walls bore museum quality aeronautical memorabilia: pictures, posters, paintings, uniforms, ribbons, awards, equipment, propellers, spars, ribs, instruments, and models – Julie's unique collection represented more than three decades in a series of positions within the airline industry. Gone were the smells of oil, fuel, and metal polishes; in their stead were the fragrant odors of meatballs, seafood canapés, crisp fried onions, fresh breads, cake, and tropical fruits. The hangar was resplendent with color and especially beautifully draped with Julie's trademark patriotic reds, whites, and blues celebrating her colorful life of service, showmanship, and performance.

As few other women can boast, Julie was retiring from one fruitful career as she rode the crest of success in her second. She was reveling in having enjoyed the best of two worlds – two worlds of her own making. It was her night to shine.

Who is Julie Clark?

As with many of us, her descriptions depend upon the persons who are answering the question. A complex, contradictory series of qualities mark most of us, qualities enhanced or constrained by those with whom we come into contact.

To her millions of air show fans, Julie is the star who is revered and applauded. She is the one they have voted into the prominent role of "favorite." She is the smooth and accomplished pilot who fearlessly proclaims her sincere patriotism for her country through her "Air Force One" aircraft's red, white, and blue paint scheme and who spends endless hours after each stirring performance signing autographs, shaking hands, answering questions, and bestowing her warm and captivating smile. She is the attraction who brings many of them out. As United Airlines' Captain Ray Hoover has stated, "If visitors go all the way to Oshkosh [Wisconsin] and see *only* Julie Clark's air show routine before going home, it is worth the trip."

To Julie's "Minnesota Mom," Gladys Hood, Julie is a sensitive, caring, responsive woman who shares intimate secrets and reveals the vulnerability characteristic of someone who has suffered tragedy and loss and who also has experienced the incredible high of having been named one of aviation's Top 100 Women of the Century by the prestigious Women in Aviation, International. To Gladys, Julie is the lovable, mercurial surrogate daughter whose enthusiasm can't be contained and whose energies propelled this normally settled friend, a saleswoman with her own antique business, into Julie's peripatetic life. Gladys said of Julie, "When I first met her, I was flabbergasted with what she'd accomplished, having to depend upon herself for everything."

To those who have loved Julie, she is a gorgeous, curvaceous, energetic, volatile, and electric bit of quicksilver – a woman desired and a woman who can't be possessed. A beauty queen and an athlete, an achiever and a determined pacesetter, Julie is a woman who can evoke the best of a man's desire to protect. Conversely, she can be feared when, like a cornered cat, she fights tooth and nail for her independence and for her busi-

With First Officer Bill Gennarelli, the captain bids farewell to a 27-year career.

ness, American Aerobatics, Inc., which she built virtually single-handedly from scratch to prominence.

To her business associates, Julie is respected as the friendly, outgoing manager of her own affairs and recognized as the sharp, skillful, and zealous guardian of her position in a competitive arena. She has celebrated seventeen years under the sponsorship of MOPAR, attesting to her demonstrated business acumen reflected in the care with which she keeps the Daimler / Chrysler name prominently displayed and long remembered. She has been deeply appreciative of long and rewarding relationships with those who have supported her with endorsements in the form of product support and those who have generously sponsored her patri-

**Julie cuts her cake
and enjoys her friends.**

otic performance. She represents their products well.

To at least one of her air show crew chiefs and perhaps more, she has been a source of inspiration. Larry Littlepage, said, "I started working with Julie in 1980 as she was beginning to get her air show business underway. It was 1989 before I decided to return to school and to pursue my own aviation career or I would still hold her crew chief position today. Thanks to Julie's encouragement, I was inspired to become a professional pilot and I currently pilot Boeing 747s for Polar Air Cargo. But, I can attest, Julie is meticulous. She runs at a high frequency. Few can sustain her levels of enthusiasm and her high energy level."

To her airline crew members, she has been the captain with whom they've flown, the capable and knowledgeable aviator who served also as a flight attendant, as a ground attendant, and purser, all of which taught her, first hand, the importance of crew coordination and mutual respect. To employees of Northwest Airlines, she represents well the profession of airline piloting and her own excellence. She brings to the cockpit a marvelous sense of humor.

Does Julie have any enemies? Perhaps there are those who have been adversely affected by someone as capable as she and perhaps some have felt jealous or resentful of her capabilities. As many employers who own and run small businesses can attest, good and devoted employees can be hard to find. Some may have failed to understand the intensity with which she attacks everything she takes on; some may not have reflected her commitment and her zeal.

There have been lovers who have been spurned; there have been friendships lost. Who among us has not experienced the same? And who among us can relish the enjoyment of having successfully achieved even one outstanding career path without having made some errors, caused some heartache? Julie has gone one better. She has been outstanding in two career fields and can receive kudos for her achievements. Perhaps some would recognize a darker side to this complex woman. Centuries ago, Virgil wrote, "...Violets are dark, too, and hyacinths."

Photo: David Poleski

Julie has suffered more in the way of personal tragedy than most. Although they have left permanent scars, she has overcome those tragedies. They have helped to steel her resolve.

Julie has faced rejection. She has made every endeavor to respond to rejection with positive improvement and a resilient attitude. She has made some poor choices and has reacted to the fall-out of poor judgment with a conscious effort to

15

improve and to survive life's inconsistencies and incongruities.

Julie has reached stardom. She has learned to accept the adulation and the attention with respectful humility. She has lived her life on her own; she has depended upon her deep faith in God and she has rallied all of her own outstanding resources toward achievement. She has adored her family members who have been so essential and important to her life. She has loved deeply, not always wisely or well. She has made mistakes, but they have been her own mistakes. She has also reached incredible levels of achievement and they, too, have been her own achievements to savor.

Who is Julie Clark?

She's the girl next door, the one you would be proud to call neighbor. She is the dancer and acrobat who shone as a gymnast and who has remained lithe and shapely throughout her life. She is the airline captain who might have been at the controls of one of your flights with Northwest Airlines – competent and cool, professional and confident. She is the entertainer who might have performed at your hometown's latest air show. She is the self-made woman, an example of femininity who is not afraid to demonstrate the strength of her convictions and the endurance of her will.

Who is Julie Clark? Read on.

CHAPTER TWO: *REMEMBERING MOM*

Marjorie Clark

Palm trees swayed in the light wind and a salty odor from San Francisco Bay permeated the 4 February 1963 morning that freshmen Julie Clark and her twin sister Judy arrived at Carlmont High School on Alameda de las Pulgas near the township line dividing San Carlos and Belmont, California. A sparse wintry fog shrouded the Santa Cruz Mountains to the west, promising to evaporate with the rising warmth of the day. Seagulls wheeled overhead, their raucous cries lost above the noise of the gathering teenagers clustered below. As frenetically as birds sought morsels of food, the high school students swarmed, searching for their closest friends.

Candy Wilson and her twin Karen shared Julie's interests in gymnastics, in cheerleading, in boys, in their classes, and in Carlmont High School athletics. Julie and Candy, especially, never lacked something to talk about and cherished the moments before class to catch up on one another's latest news. Because their teachers had to separate them in class to cut down on their irrepressible enthusi-

Julie, left, and Judy Clark, at three months

asm and chatter, meeting before school was a favorite ritual.

When the opening bell rang, the noise funneled into the hallways with the clusters of students; halls resounded with their eager banter and with the slamming of locker doors. As home rooms filled, the halls slowly quieted and emptied. They fell silent and gray.

This particular winter morning hadn't been any different than the day before. As was their custom, Julie and Judy used their own alarm clocks to rouse themselves from bed and they dashed into the kitchen where their father, Ernie Clark, a Captain with Pacific Air Lines, fixed their breakfasts. His scheduled flight didn't leave until almost noon. Their older sister, Sharon, a freshman at San Jose State College, was home on break and was still in her room.

Marjorie Clark

Their mother, Marjorie Johnson Clark, was following her normal routine as well. More of a night owl, she tended to stay up into the late evenings. When morning awakened the rest of the family on days that her husband had no flights planned, Marge liked to sleep in.

Marge was a classy woman. A lover of pretty clothes, she dressed impeccably, wore her hair beautifully coifed, painted her nails, and put on makeup before she felt ready for her day. She was popular and outgoing and she had an irrepressible and contagious laugh so endearing to her many friends. A caring mother, Marge was a mentor to her three daughters. Julie recalled, "If we looked sloppily dressed, she'd admonish us, 'You know we're not downtown. Put on a blouse or something nice.' She always saw to it that we girls reflected her feminine and attractive style."

Like many wives of the 1950s and early 1960s, Marge Clark was a homemaker – the one who was home when the girls came in from elementary school, the one who listened to their delights and commiserated with their disappointments. As her daughters grew, she studied to become a licensed realtor and took a job with Frater's Realty. Julie recalled, "Every time we girls were home and heard the sounds of fire engines, we'd glance at one another and know the telephone was about to ring. Our Mom never failed to call home at the sound of sirens, checking to ensure that the dispatched rescue squad wasn't headed for our home. It almost became a joke."

Like many of the same era, too, she enjoyed alcoholic drinks every evening and she smoked cigarettes, as did most of the stars of the silver screen. However, Julie told that, when Marge took them out to dinner when Ernie was flying, she would light a cigarette at the end of the meal and, while pointing her glowing ash at first one and then the others in rhythm with her admonishment, she chastised her daughters with, "I hope none of you will ever start this dirty, nasty, expensive habit."

They'd invariably repeat, with a smile, "We know, Mom; it's a 'dirty, nasty, expensive habit.'"

Most of Ernie's and Marge's friends were pilots and most flew for Pacific Air Lines. Marge fit gracefully into their cocktail party circuit and was active in the bridge club made up of airline pilots' wives. She had an especially close-knit group of friends.

Respecting their mother's wishes

Judy, Julie, and Sharon at home

to be left alone on the mornings that Ernie enjoyed fixing breakfast for the girls, Julie and Judy generally crept quietly through Marge's bedroom to her adjoining bathroom to use her hair spray. This morning, as they had so routinely done, the two tiptoed into her room, leaving the hallway light off so the brightness wouldn't wake her.

As they slipped out, they heard labored sounds from her bed. "Was Mom snoring?" Julie wondered. Not wanting to disturb her, she and Judy dashed into the kitchen, kissed goodbyes to their dad, and rushed off to school.

Now they were in their home rooms, the day stretching before them. Julie waited for the bell to signal the change of classes for first period.

Instead of a class bell, the classroom phone rang. Her teacher took the call, then turned gravely and walked to Julie's desk. "Julie, you'll have to gather your books and go to the office."

To the office? I have to go to the office?

"Take everything with you. You won't be coming back to class," her teacher added. Julie glanced at Candy and shrugged her shoulders. *I won't be coming back? What on earth?*

The same hallway that had reverberated with the sounds of laughter closed around her, evincing a gloomy silence. When Judy came out of her classroom, the twins stared at each other. "You have to go to the office, too? This is weird. What is this all about? We've never been sent to the principal's office in our lives!"

As soon as the office door opened, three of Julie's mother's friends stood inside, their faces mirroring tragedy: Katie Couk, Myrt McBride, and Polly Geraci. Katie's husband, Rudy Couk, was another pilot for Pacific Air Lines and Ernie Clark's closest friend. Myrt had known Marge and Ernie from their first dating days. Polly and her husband, Dr. Charlie Geraci, a medical doctor who took care of every member of the family, lived across the street from the Clarks.

Someone spoke in a low voice. It was unreal; to Julie, time warped. The scene lapsed into slow motion and she felt like an observer to a charade. Through muffled words, she heard someone mention Marge.

"I heard them telling me my mother had choked to death. Mom was gone. *Gone!*" she said. "I couldn't believe them. I couldn't believe that it was possible. She was only forty-four! She had everything to *live* for. I wanted them to be wrong! I wanted to scream. I wanted them to be wrong, terribly, dreadfully *wrong!*"

By the time the sobbing girls were driven home, emergency crews had taken Marge away and the house, normally warm and inviting, was forbidding. Even worse, it was cluttered to overflowing with somber people whose dismal faces and whispered voices reflected the extent of the tragedy. Ernie sat on the living room couch, holding his head in his hands.

Luckily, Sharon was there to hug the twins close. Although she, too, felt intense grief, she summoned amazing strength and helped Ernie and her sisters through the tragic ordeal. They appreciated the support of friends, but found their greatest comfort in one another. They wished for nothing more than that the day could start again. That an impossibility, they fervently wished to be left alone.

Julie said, "I had never seen my father cry. Now he broke down and sobbed. He was devastated.

"We all missed Mom horribly, but it was particularly hard to watch the toll it took on Dad. Sometimes, he would put his arms around me and cry as if his heart would break. He missed Mom a lot and suffered so very much."

Emotions Ran High

Guilt hung heavily on Ernie's and Julie and her sisters' shoulders. *What if they'd said something about the 'snoring' they'd heard that fateful morning? What if someone had turned on the light and checked on her before it was too late? What if Ernie had been scheduled to fly earlier, had gone in to kiss her goodbye, and had found Marge in time? What if?! What if?!*

Memories tossed in their heads like waves crashing on a California beach. Julie remembered having her father come in from airline trips, his uniform hat perched jauntily on his head. He'd grab Marge in a hug and give her a kiss, and then she'd knock his hat onto the floor, laughing. The girls would say, "You guys, quit the

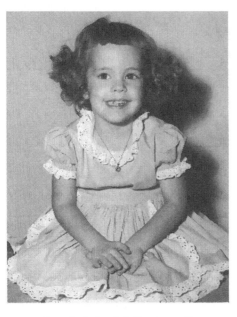
A curly-haired Julie at age three

mushy stuff. We're eating…"

Ernie would turn to the girls to say, "Excuse me, please; I just want to have my ration with your Mom."

Worse, Julie remembered the night before. Having been warned not to eat gooey sweets while wearing braces on her teeth, her mom had caught her taking bites of a rich brownie. Angrily, Marge swatted the brownie out of Julie's hand, saying, "You know better than to eat that!" Julie had dashed from the room in tears. Later, in the dark of night, Marge had come into Julie's room and bent over her bed. Julie admitted, "I was awake, but I pretended to be asleep. Mom said, 'I'll always love you,' as she bent over to kiss me on the cheek. I kept my eyes closed, but I felt a little smile play across my lips. All I could wonder later was whether she had seen my smile. Maybe it put everything right between us before her death."

The Sign of Sagittarius

Marjorie Clark had been born on 27 November 1918. A Sagittarian, she had many of the attributes attributed to those born under the sign of the Archer. She was optimistic and freedom-loving, honest, good-humored, jovial, and full of energy. She also shared some of their flaws, being apt to flare up in anger over trivial things and tending to be restless and impatient.

Julie recalled, "They had a good marriage, but Mom sometimes had a dreadful temper. I remember her throwing a cast-iron pan filled with spaghetti sauce at my dad. It missed, splattering against the interior brick wall of our kitchen. Later, he would point out the 'battle scars,' stains remaining despite repeated scrubbings. He always laughed and said, 'Luckily, I ducked!'

"And I used to dread when Dad was away on trips. Mom didn't drink a lot, but she drank more when Dad was away. Sometimes she'd get 'pissy' and we three girls would ask each other, 'Is this going to be a bad evening?' She would go on rampages. Once she stormed into our rooms to see if our dresser drawers were clean and tidy. She yanked out the drawers and dumped everything on the floor before ordering, 'Now, clean it up!'"

Sharon, Julie, and Judy Clark

Much more often, Marjorie Johnson Clark was a loving mother to her daughters. She had given birth to Sharon in January 1945 and, on 27 June 1948, fraternal twins Julie Elizabeth, at five pounds and ten ounces, and Judy Ann, at six pounds and three ounces, were born. The birth announcement stated, "We're TWO reasons our Mommy and Daddy are happy. Folks are making quite a fuss since they found out there's TWO of us."

The Clarks' home had been designed by Simmons and Simmons and built by George Pryor, both firms of Menlo Park, California. The ranch-style house perched high on Knoll Drive on the eastern slopes of the Santa Cruz Mountains and offered a view carrying the eye to San Francisco Bay. It nestled in San Carlos, which lies against the foothills directly south and slightly east of San Francisco, in the midst of today's Silicon Valley. With many physicians living on Knoll Drive,

23

Ernie used to tease, "It should be called, 'Pill Hill.'"

Marge often said, with more than a hint of pride in her voice, "You should see the view from our living room at night."

Julie explained, "We could look all the way across the Bay and see Oakland. City lights shimmered on the water and blended with the flickering reflections of the moon."

Often included in Home Tours, their house boasted the huge brick fireplace, still bearing the reminders of the thrown spaghetti pot. The fireplace reached thirteen feet to the ceiling and faced the kitchen as well as the family room. In the kitchen, the brick held an electric oven. From the family room rear access, barbecuing was possible.

The four bedroom and two-and-a-half bath home was complemented by a swimming pool in the back yard. Ernie often teased, in a loving way, "*I* wanted to buy an airplane, but Marge wanted a swimming pool."

"I think Dad did his best to give Mom everything she wanted," said Julie. "He adored her."

**A pride in their
daughters shows in the faces of Marjorie and Ernie Clark.
They wanted the best for all three.**

Julie's Baby Book

Marge Clark kept a baby book for each of her three children. Enclosed in Julie's baby book was a picture of Mrs. Laurie Harper of Lavington, Australia, with her seven children, all born within four years. Four-year-old Garry Harper was followed by three sets of twins born in a period of two-and-a-half years. Perhaps Marge kept her energy level high by glancing at that photograph when times were harried with her single set of twins.

A copy of the birth certificate named Julie's parents formally: Born in Hayward Hospital to Ernest Ashcroft Clark, Jr., of Omaha, Nebraska, and Marjorie Edith Johnson Clark of Minneapolis, Minnesota. The attending physician was Doctor Samuel Gersten.

Most telling of Marge's love was written in her own hand. In Julie's baby book she wrote, "Dear Julie, Mommy and Daddy will never, never forget the day 'Our Twins' were born. My! How sweet you both are, and you with that curly hair. This is a wonderful and very interesting experience. Taking care of two of you at once is a lot of work. But, you both are definitely in the 'Good Baby Class.' And we sure do love you. Sharon thinks having two babies in the family is grand and we all do for that matter. Love, your Mother."

Marge noted, "First photo taken by Daddy, at Home, July 1948," and entered, "Pets and best loved Playthings: Sharon's dolls, a Baton, an Easter bunny on wheels, a sand bucket, paper and pencil, and a paper bag filled with treasures – Julie even took it to bed."

She wrote, "When Julie and Judy were seven months old – on 4 January 1949 – they came down with chicken pox. Just two weeks had elapsed since four-year-old Sharon had broken out with them."

Then she added, "Julie shows very little desire for physical activity. She wants more than anything to be loved and to love little tiny toys."

Under: *Sweet Things to Remember*: "Julie seems so clothes conscious, even at 14 months. When you put a pretty dress on her, she holds it up and looks at it as if to say, "My, isn't this a lovely dress?""

"Julie's First Sentence: 'Down she goes!' at 22 months. She's twirling a baton at 23 months and really doing it to perfection. She's saying 'Hi' to strangers and being very friendly."

Under First Birthday, "Julie Beth and Judy Ann had a grand birthday together, although I believe Sharon, Daddy, and Mommy enjoyed it a lot more. We had an angel food cake, cut in half and decorated in pink and rose. Each half had one candle on it and each had their names: Julie Beth and Judy Ann."

A year later she wrote: "Julie didn't care for the birthday cake, but ate lots of ice cream. … (Sharon had a broken arm and was just getting over the mumps!)"

For the Second Christmas, "Julie was afraid of all the toys and wouldn't touch them for weeks. Loved the Christmas tree, though."

And, in 1950, the third Christmas, Marge wrote, "Julie loved Christmas this year and loved playing with the doll beds and dolls that she and Judy both received. Was much impressed with her new clothes, too. Our first Christmas at 1305 Morse Blvd, San Carlos."

A complex woman, Marjorie Clark evoked trepidation and unease as well as respect and admiration in Julie. When Marge lost her temper, Julie did her utmost to stay out of her way. Primarily, however, Julie felt close to her mother. She knew Marge wanted nothing but the best for her and for everyone in the family. She was an excellent cook and insisted upon her daughters being home for dinner each evening and focused on the time for the family to share. She made holiday dinners the special events that she felt them to be, decorating the table with delightful arrangements and ensuring that she and her girls were beautifully dressed, as well. Marge was a rock around which the family was anchored; she was a loving mother who was taken when Julie needed her the most.

CHAPTER THREE: *HER HERO, HER DAD*

Sunday mornings was one Marge's favorite days. She led the way, waking early to get her family fed, dressed, and ready for church. The Clarks attended an Episcopal church and, while the girls went to their respective classes, Ernie ushered parishioners and Marge taught a Sunday School class. Later, in the silence of the chancel after having lost her mother, fourteen-year-old Julie prayed for her and

Ernie Clark

fervently prayed for the safety of her father, "Please, God. Take care of my dad. Please keep him safe." Her father was her *hero*.

Ernie Clark would have been the last person to call himself a hero. Self-effacing and low-key, he felt fortunate to earn a living in the field he loved most – flying. He was humble and patient, easy-going and witty.

He would have said, "Hero? Not I."

But, to his adoring daughter Julie, he was definitely a hero.

Ernie Clark

In 1929, two years after *his* hero, Charles Lindbergh, soloed across the Atlantic Ocean, a youthful Ernest A. "Bud" Clark made giant strides toward his goal of taking wing. He was the winner of an essay contest designed to contribute to the air-mindedness of his home town of Omaha, Nebraska and its sister city, Council Bluffs, Iowa.

Ernie titled his essay, "How To Make Omaha and Council Bluffs the Aviation Center of the United States," and he suggested "building an airport complete with lighting for night flying, hangars for the planes, machine shop operations, a weather station, a street railway that would schedule bus lines to carry passengers to the airfield, and, an aircraft show similar to our annual auto show designed to bring a great many citizens to the desired state of air-mindedness." In his wildest imagination, Ernie could not have pictured *his* daughter starring in air shows at just such airports throughout the United States and Canada.

But, still a teenager himself, Ernie owed thanks to the Thomas Alva Edison Scholarship program contest for his wonderful prize of ten hours of flight training. He started his lessons immediately, becoming a licensed student pilot on 16 July 1929. His flight instructor, Cliff Burham, who had flown his first airplane, a Monoprep, into Council Bluffs in 1919, shared his love of aviation with his protégé and Ernie Clark proved an eager pupil. Ernie soloed in five hours and one more totally committed pilot joined the annals of aviation history.

Not simply content to know how to fly, Ernie became the youngest person in Omaha to own his own airplane. He paid $35 in cash and worked off $65 in welding to purchase a Swallow biplane that was no better than a "heap." It required a complete rebuilding and a replacement engine. Ernie saved his cash and spent $65 to buy an OX-5 engine requiring as much repair as the plane itself. With dogged persistence, a determined Ernie shaped and repaired his airplane to airworthiness. The complex construction consumed him until his craft was completed and airworthy. Tested in the craft that bore his workmanship, Ernie became a private pilot on 30 September 1936. He received his Transport license on 28 June 1937.

Ernie had been born on 1 January 1912 to Emily Brown Clark and the father for whom he was named, Ernest Ashcroft Clark. Tragically, the senior E.A. Clark died when his son, Ernie, was three years old, and his daughter, Dorothy, was six. Emily struggled to care for her children and Ernie never lost his affection and admiration for his mother. He also never lost his passion for the skies.

Having inspired two others of his friends, Bob Donnell, a pilot, and Charles Branstetter, a mechanic, the trio accepted the challenge of setting record flights. Bob Donnell and Ernie tried their hands at endurance. Calling them the "Stay Up Flight" and the "Flight to Nowhere," Ernie and Bob Donnell set endurance flight records of: 20 hrs, 56 minutes on 31 Aug 39 and 4 days 1 hour and 30 minutes on 5 Sep 39. The trio received fan mail. Ernie joked about one of his letters, addressed to "Dopey Clark!" and told his daughters someone must have figured he really was dopey to make such piloting attempts. The men represented all who had been imbued with the contagious competitive spirit of aviation. However, tympani beats of war sounded across the Atlantic Ocean and swelled toward a fever pitch as what would become World War II erupted with Hitler's arrogance on one hand and Roosevelt's and Churchill's fury on the other.

Ever the U.S. patriot, Ernie enlisted in the Army Reserve and soon wore the wings of the World War II U.S. Army Air Corps (USAAC), flying C-47s in the Air Transport Command. As a Transport Pilot, he flew out of Kansas City with Mid-Continent Airlines, which responded to the war effort and transported troops to and from their places of embarkation. Mid-Continent merged in 1952 with Braniff, which became Braniff International; but, the merger did not come before Ernie had met and fallen in love with a lovely clerical employee of Mid-Continent Airlines – Marjorie Johnson. Ernie and Marjorie were married in November 1943. Mr. L. Homer Mouden was the pilot and enduring friend who introduced Ernie to Marjorie. At the age of 91 and 31 years after his retirement as an airline pilot, Homer wrote to Julie, "We have followed your career throughout the years and have been proud to have been a part of your life since you were born." The Moudens were part of Julie's life since *before* she was born.

In 1944, Ernie was transferred to Long Beach, California where his and Marge's first daughter, Sharon, was born on 4 January 1945. By 5 May 1945 Ernie was transferred to Stockton, California and he was honorably discharged from the United States Army Air Corps on 3 November 1945. He and Marge opted to move to Rio Linda, California, where his Aunt and Uncle Hesselink had purchased a chicken ranch. Though Ernie made every effort to adapt to becoming a chicken farmer and to help his uncle in *his* choice of occupations, farming was

Judy, Sharon, and Julie go flying from Oakland with their dad.

light years from Ernie's idea of making a living. He much preferred the thoughts of winging his way through the sky.

Later, as his wife Marge told it, if the sounds of an aircraft engine pulled his eyes skyward while he was in the midst of shoveling manure, he would stop in his tracks to gaze forlornly at the sky. Marge finally asked him, "Ernie, what are we *doing* here?" To hear Marge recognize he wasn't cut out to be a chicken farmer was exactly

the push he needed.

Ernie contacted some acquaintances and, in 1947, he, Marge, and Sharon left Rio Linda for San Lorenzo, California to help create the line that became

Ernie Clark's Pacific Air Lines

Southwest Airways – the line proudly bearing a large Thunderbird logo on its Douglas DC-3 aircraft tails. Ernie, hired as a captain, was one of the line's original thirty pilots and proud to be one of the "Dirty Thirty," as they became known.

Southwest becomes Pacific

Southwest Airways, a scheduled airline that opened its doors to passengers in 1946, was California's own. It operated throughout the state through 1958 when routes began to stretch beyond the state's borders and the airline's name changed to Pacific Air Lines. The logo was modernized and the headquarters of the operation moved to San Francisco, taking Ernie and Marge along with it. The Clarks relocated in Hayward, California in 1948 in time for their twins to be born.

Ernie initially piloted Douglas DC-3s and then he moved to Martin 4-0-4s, forty-passenger pressurized airliners powered by two Pratt and Whitney R-2800 piston engines. Martin 4-0-4s flew at 280 miles per hour. Pacific Air Lines had purchased its Martins from Eastern and TWA. Given one unique chance to pilot a jet airliner, he flew a Caravelle on 11 June 1957, but his primary mounts became Fokker F.27 turbo-jets. These mid-sized, high-wing aircraft designed by the Netherlands' Fokker Aircraft company carried 36 to 40 passengers. Powered by two Rolls-Royce Dart turbo-prop engines and known as the F.27 *Friendship*, the first flew in November of 1955. Fokker's design was licensed to be built in the United States by the Fairchild Industries and its name was changed almost imperceptibly from F.27 to the hyphenated F-27.

The establishment as a new classification in 1944 by the Civil Aeronautics Board (CAB) of "Feeder Airlines" led to the growth of small lines like Pacific. In part, Pacific and other small airlines grew because the areas they served held a widespread population and traveling distances were great. Ernie Clark rode on the swell of this burgeoning airline and reveled in his good luck. From the soil to the sky, he was so drastically removed from shoveling manure; he must have felt elated to return to the sky.

"Top Banana of the West"

From Heights to Depths

Yet, Marge's death left an aching void. In addition to her intimacy and love, Ernie had always counted on Marge seeing to the house, taking care of the girls, making sure meals were on the table, the shopping was done, schoolwork was monitored, and the household was running smoothly when he went away on trips. Marge had been his companion, his friend, his love. Devastated to have lost her, he was deeply troubled about how to go on, how to care for his children, and how to see they were raised as he and Marge wanted.

In the afternoons, as Julie came into the house from school, she, too, found her mother's absence unbearable. Gone were the moments they'd shared. Gone was the chance to burst in with the news of school and have it fall on interested ears. Gone was the woman who set an example for her and gave her character qualities she could emulate if she wanted, rebel against if necessary.

Finally, Ernie admitted, "I just can't live with all the memories this house holds. Let's talk about where you would go to school if we were to move."

Julie thought, "Move? We've lived here so *long*, Our house is so pretty. It's Knoll Drive; it's *home*."

Nonetheless, the girls recognized their father's acute grief and the need for all of them to think of the future. Even the faded red spaghetti sauce stain on the brick wall kept open wounds that needed to heal. It was important for Ernie to start again and go on with life; the girls recognized it would give them new starts

- -

32

as well. Selling the Knoll Drive home, he bought a home at 151 Alberta Avenue, allowing Julie and Judy to attend their school of choice, San Carlos High School.

A Blessing

Then their father made another suggestion. "I want to contact your Aunt Dorothy. You know she's the only relative I have and, as my only sister and a widow, I think she would be a good woman to have living here with us."

The girls agreed it would be great to have Dorothy around and it was fortunate she was not only able to come, but that she was eager and willing to share their lives. Dorothy Clark Hawley, who was about 56 at the time, was gracious and loving – a wonderful influence upon them all.

Julie remembered, "She was a member of Eastern Star, to which she was devoted. We liked watching her swish out of the house in fancy evening dresses. She also loved to tell us stories about our Dad when he was young. She was proud of all her little brother had accomplished. Dorothy had been especially pleased Dad

Captain Ernie Clark

had let her do some of the rib-stitching on the fabric of his first airplane and that he had given her a small set of his Air Force wings.

"She loved to repeat the stories of Dad's endurance flights, especially the flight that lasted *four days* plus one hour and a half! If Dad walked in while Dorothy was regaling us with these exploits, he'd laugh and remind us that he and his buddies called it, 'Flight to Nowhere.'

"We couldn't understand why *anyone* would want to fly circles in the sky for such a long time."

The family was struggling, but they were getting their emotions under control. They were forcing themselves to look to the future. The ache was irreparable; it was permanent. It would *never* go away. But, fortunately for Julie, high school activities consumed most of the weekdays and, on weekends, as a San Carlos high school junior and a cheerleader, it was important for her to show great school spirit. She threw herself into energetic gymnastics at the school's competitive games, rallying the fans from her school. It was good to be busy and involved.

No End to Despair

Then, on 7 May 1964, Julie was called out of her class and told to report to the principal's office. "No!" she wanted to scream. Icy fingers of fear cramped her stomach. Bile coursed through her body and she found it nearly impossible to stumble out of the class and into the bleak and empty hall. She was torn with an excruciating anxiety. When her twin sister Judy appeared, her face drawn and worried, the high school hallway grew icy. Suddenly dark and forbidding, the gray walls started closing in. It was as if breath was sucked from their lungs. Their footsteps echoed in the hall, suddenly a hall from hell.

"This can't be happening," Julie gasped. "There has to be some mistake. This just can't be true!"

As Julie neared the principal's office, the group of anguished women was gathered as they had faced her only fifteen months before. She screamed an eerie, keening cry. She yelled, "No! No!" and began sobbing hysterically.

Her worst fears were realized. On 7 May 1964, her father, Captain Ernie Clark, his co-pilot Raymond Andress, a flight attendant, Margaret Shafer, and forty innocent passengers were killed tragically and senselessly when a crazed gunman pushed into the cockpit and shot both pilots at the controls of their twin-engined F-27. It was a grim, terrifying murder, a gruesome harbinger of deaths to innocents. It was the first, but not the only such horror in U.S. airliner history.

Even more heartrending was the fact Ernie Clark hadn't been the scheduled pilot for that particular flight. He had filled in for a pilot who had called in sick.

A Terrifying Reality

An accident report was filed by Pacific Air Lines and adopted on 28 October 1964 by the Civil Aeronautics Board, Washington, D.C. Released 2 November 1964, the report stated:

"...A search of the wreckage area disclosed the presence of a .357 Smith and Wesson Model 27 Magnum revolver (S/N S210645), containing six empty cartridges that had been fired by the weapon. It had a broken frame, jammed cylinder, and missing pistol grips. Human tissue was adhering to it. Clothing fibers were embedded in and adhering to the tissue.

"The gun with ammunition and a cleaning kit had been purchased by passenger Francisco Paula Gonzales on the evening of 6 May 1964. Gonzales had advised friends and relatives that he would die on either Wednesday, 6 May or Thursday, 7 May. He referred to his impending death on a daily basis throughout the week preceding the accident. On the evening of 6 May, passenger Gonzales departed SFO International Airport aboard a Pacific Air Lines (PAL) flight for Reno, Nevada with a return reservation for Flight 773 on the following morning. Shortly before boarding the flight to Reno, Gonzales displayed the gun to numerous friends at the airport and told one person he intended to shoot himself. Various persons saw Gonzales board the PAL flight at San Francisco Airport (SFO) carrying the small package that contained the gun and ammunition. That same evening, he had purchased two insurance policies at the SFO airport in the total amount of $105,000. Another passenger aboard the flight from SFO to RNO recalled that Gonzales was carrying a small package and was seated in the front seat behind the pilots' compartment. While in Reno, Gonzales spent the night visiting various gambling establishments. He gambled and one casino employee asked how he was doing to which Gonzales replied, '...it would not make any difference after tomorrow.' Several persons recalled that he had a large bulge in his clothing and others reported that he was carrying a small package while in Reno. A janitor at a gambling club where Gonzales was known to have spent part of the evening discovered a cardboard carton for a Smith and Wesson Magnum revolver and a gun cleaning kit in the wastepaper container. Both were identified by the seller as part of passenger Gonzales' purchase on the previous evening.

"Interviews with relatives, associates, and acquaintances revealed that Gonzales was disturbed and depressed over marital and financial difficulties and had cried continuously during the evening of 5 May 1964. A credit check showed him to have been deeply in debt and that nearly half of his salary was committed for loan payments.

"A read-out of the flight recorder tape indicated that the flight was normal from takeoff at 0638 until approximately 10 minutes after departure from [an intermediate stop at] Stockton. At this time, the recorder traces indicated the aircraft was cruising at 5,000 feet indicated altitude on a magnetic heading of approximately 230 degrees and at an airspeed of approximately 213 knots. The first erratic indications on the tape appeared commensurate with the high-pitched transmission by the copilot, which occurred at 0648:15 AM. At this point on the flight recorder tape, the four traces for altitude, airspeed, heading, and acceleration began to make sharp positive excursions. The altitude trace began a sharp excursion indicating a descent from 5,300 to 2,100 feet within 22.5 seconds or at a descent rate of approximately 9,000 feet per minute. During the same time interval, the airspeed trace indicated an increase to 335 knots and the heading trace indicated a change to approximately 265 degrees. The vertical acceleration trace indicated a decrease first to approximately minus 0.4G and then an increase to plus 2.5Gs during the same period.

"The altitude trace then indicated a climb to approximately 3,200 feet in 15 seconds or at a rate of 4,400 feet per minute, during which the airspeed trace indicated a decrease to approximately 265 knots. The heading continued a change to approximately 285 degrees. Vertical acceleration continued to vary from plus 2.5Gs to minus 0.4G. From this point to the end of the recorded tracings, all traces were abnormal.

"The transmission and the flight recorder recorded a momentary interruption in the dive 22 seconds after it began and were the only indications of the flight crews' actions during the final minute of flight. This evidence does not furnish sufficient parameters to determine a specific time point at which both pilots became completely incapacitated. Bullet indentations were found in the rear structure of Captain Clark's seat.

"...Captain Ernest A. Clark, age 52, held valid airline transport pilot certificate No. 33313 with type ratings in Douglas DC-3, Martin 202/404, and Fairchild F-27 aircraft. His physical qualifications were current and without waivers. He originally qualified in the F-27 on 10 March 1959. He had 20,434:12 flying hours of which 2,793:40 hours were in F-27 aircraft. His last proficiency check in F-27 aircraft was on 8 September 1963."

News Headlines

"Craft Nose Dives into Foothills Near Mt. Diablo."

"East Bay Airplane Tragedy."

"Murder in the sky." This crash made news reports throughout the world.

In famed aviation writer Robert Serling's book, *Loud and Clear,* a compassionate Serling quoted from *Newsweek.* He wrote, "*Newsweek's National Affairs* reported, 'The last garbled words over the radio: 'Skipper's shot! We've been shot,' were followed by a scream, perhaps from co-pilot Raymond Andress, perhaps from someone else. Then the tape ended.

"...The FBI entered the case. [It] traced the weapon to a San Francisco area man who bought more insurance than any other passenger – in excess of $50,000. They pieced together the story: the man entered the crew compartment through the unlocked door. Once inside, he shot the pilot, co-pilot, and perhaps the stewardess Margaret Schafer, and one or more passengers who tried to intervene. He might have fired the magnum, an unusually powerful weapon that can knock a man down at 50 yards, into the left motor, which subsequently went dead.

"A San Francisco Examiner story said the man who owned the gun and bought the insurance was Frank Gonzales, 27, a Filipino who had been a member of his country's 1960 Olympic yachting team. Returning from Naples after the Games, he stopped off in San Francisco and decided to live there permanently. Married and with a baby son, his marriage failed. Despondent about the marriage breakup, Gonzales seemed, according to his brother James, to have conflicting currents in his personality.

"He made frequent gambling trips to Nevada and bought the gun from a man in Riverside, California. In Reno, he mailed a last gift to his small son and purchased insurance policies for several members of his family, policies that will be worthless if it can be proved that he fired the shots that caused the crash.

"The aircraft crashed with explosive force, snuffing out the lives of [whoever remained alive of the] forty passengers and three crewmembers. If a joint investigation of the FBI and FAA confirms the belief that a gunman killed the crew, it would be the first such case of its kind in U.S. aviation history.

"...Frank Gonzales had shot both men from behind and he had gratified his demented wish to die that day in a horrifying act of multiple murder."

Unspeakable Horror

The aviation-savvy Serling projected a voice that accurately and empathetically related to the air and to airmen. This was not true of all reporters. Invariably, the newspaper articles, governmental reports, and the dispassionate drone of news anchors were sensationalized and lurid. Before the complete analysis of the crash was made public, rumors flew that erroneously intimated that Ernie was despondent over his wife's death and that he might have been to blame for the crash. It was an agonizing and dreadful period in Julie's life. To some reporters, too, this accident report served as a greedy sales tool to elevate ratings, to lure the ghoulish who seemed drawn to fire engines, ambulances, police chases, and worse, to fiery, fatal air disasters like moths are drawn to light.

To Julie, this was Dad, a man who lived up to the best qualities of those born under the sign of Capricorn. He was ambitious, determined, disciplined, patient, humorous, practical, and reserved. Known to persist toward goals with unstinting effort, Ernie typified those who respect discipline from superiors and demand it from those for whom they are responsible. As Capricorn traits include fatalism, perhaps Ernie pursued his life without concern for his own safety, worrying only about his wife, his daughters, and those passengers whose lives depended upon his safety and success as a pilot. He would have despised the taking of innocent lives in this heinous act.

The airplane crashed on rolling land and, had Gonzales committed his evil a scant eight minutes later, it might have gone down in San Francisco Bay. There the evidence might have been lost forever. The gun might not have been retrieved and the examination of the wreckage would have been sorely compromised at best.

In a premeditated murder, Gonzales pulled the trigger and killed innocent people in a location that left the record of his crimes. Unknown to him, but important to those who captain aircraft, he ensured that the ubiquitous label of "pilot error" would NOT be ascribed to this particular tragedy.

Forty innocent passengers were murdered just as plainly as Ernie, his co-pilot, and the flight attendant were murdered. The twenty-seven year old passenger who took their lives was depressed. Yet, Julie asked herself, repeatedly, "Why didn't he just shoot himself? Why did he have to ruin the lives of so many others?"

Co-pilot Ray Andress, of Santa Clara and then 31, left a wife, Martha, three daughters, Anita, 9; Audrey, 8; and Allison, 4; and a son, Steven, who was only two years old. Margaret "Margie" Schafer of Belmont left a daughter Michelle, a sixth grader. Ernie Clark left an aching void by orphaning his three girls. He and the others were far more than mere impersonal and calculated statistics. Later, the rule requiring cockpit doors to be locked on commercial U.S. airliners was named for Ernie Clark. That came *way* too late and was of small comfort.

This was Julie's *hero*, her beloved *father*, the most important man in her life, the one whose approval mattered more to her than anyone else's would ever matter. This was an irreparable wound, a recollection impossible to be erased, not with time nor faith nor prayer.

Somehow, she would find life worth living. In some way, she would put her life on track and get on with her hopes and dreams. This is what her mother and father would have wanted. This was the least she could do to honor her parents.

But, what lay ahead?

Comfort and joy lay ahead, in the same skies
Ernie had flown, the same skies Ernie had loved.

CHAPTER FOUR: *EXPLORATION*

**Julie, during her Pom-Pon days
at San Carlos High School**

It was tough enough to be teenagers during "The Sixties," the era reeking with the burning hemp of marijuana, resounding to its own percussive beat, and urging people to "find themselves" with the use of hallucinatory and illegal drugs and way-out behavior. This decade encouraged rebellion against the established societal rules, authority, ethics, codes of behavior, and taunted, "If it feels good, *Do* it!" Idealistic and restless teenagers were particularly susceptible.

Now here were three young women having to face their future without the parental love, discipline, and guidance they *knew* Ernie and Marge would have generously given. Agonizing questions would have been torment enough. *"What is going to happen to us? What are we going to do? How are we going to get along? Do we have money? Do we have to move? Might we be separated?"* The thoughts cut like knives.

"After Dad's accident," Julie said, "our house was filled with people. Aunt Dorothy was the rock we depended on and Sharon was a tower of strength; but, I used to run and hide behind the toilet in a locked bathroom to avoid all who tried to be kind and ended up congesting our home, our meals, and our privacy. Members of the press, well aware three *orphans* lived in the home, were relentless. Reporters camped in our front yard for three weeks, playing the orphan angle in a big way and thrusting microphones into our faces any time we tried to leave home to reestablish some sort of normal routine."

Loss of their parents was tragic enough. The sorrowful girls didn't need the ubiquitous and aggressive behavior of reporters to remind them. Along with Sharon and Judy, of *course* Julie struggled with her sorrow. She didn't need, want, or ask for the unforgettable and unforgivable treatment by a phalanx of paparazzi. She could see them out of a window late at night or early in the morning, exuding their blackness, hovering like cloying leeches, biding their time until a front or a back door opened and they could thrust microphones into her face or pop flash pictures of "one of the orphans."

A Shaken Faith

"As far as I was concerned, when Dad was killed, my life ended. I was devastated. For a long time, I didn't pray; I didn't go to church.

"My nights were wracked with nightmares. I dreamed – and *believed* the dreams in the light of day – I was going to have to quit school and go to work in a hardware store. Over and over, I dreamed leaving school. I woke up crying."

The Episcopal Church to which the Clarks belonged erected attractive gates around the altar. They were dedicated to Marjorie and Ernest Clark and, with the Alpha and the Omega, represented eternal life. It took Julie a long time before she could stand to enter the church and to see those gates without a fresh set of tears streaming from her eyes.

School, too, presented its own set of challenges. Julie said, "You realize you have to get on with your life, but the hardest thing about dealing with death is facing the sympathy and pity in people's eyes. You find yourself sympathetic with *them* because so many are uncomfortable and have no idea what to say or do about *your* loss. Some of them say nothing, having no idea of what to say. Some of them say something, just to open a conversation. Announcements blared over the high school's public address system. Even individual teachers stated, 'We want to welcome Julie back. She has had a rough time.'

"I wanted to say, 'Oh, just don't say *anything.*' Yet, I'm not sure what I expected or what I wanted them to say or do. The whole hideous reality was a ghastly new experience. No one wants to be ignored; but so often I yearned that the horror of it all wouldn't rear its ugly head each and every time I walked into a room, or saw a friend, or joined a group."

Later, a man approached Julie at a neighborhood gathering. He said, "You're Julie Clark, aren't you? Your dad was killed in an F-27." He paused, and then added, "I was the pilot of the United Airlines' flight who reported black smoke coming up through the undercast when the controllers lost radar contact with your dad's airplane. We confirmed it must have been a crash."

What does a grieving daughter say in response? What *can* be said?

Later, she had the chance to fly as a first officer with Captain Lou Dorflinger, a pilot friend of her father. During the flight, Lou said to Julie, "God. I just loved your dad."

Julie recalled, "We were on a DC-9 flight out of San Francisco and over Klamath Falls, Oregon, and en route to Boise, Idaho." During their conversation, Julie mentioned the pilot who had called in sick on the day her dad had died.

In a very quiet voice, Lou said, "I was that man, Julie."

"I was stunned!" said Julie. "He didn't have to tell me. He could have stayed quiet and I never would have known. But, he must have agonized over the fateful crash.

"He went on, 'You cannot possibly know how much I have struggled with this. But, I want you to know, I wasn't just out on a golf course. I was truly sick.'"

The reminders came when they were least expected. Each time the wound tore open as painfully as it had on 7 May 1964. It would *never* go away.

Another Nadir

Yet, the depths had not yet been reached. Ernie Clark's will stipulated, according to a prior agreement between Julie's parents, the guardians of Sharon, Judy, and Julie were to be Arlene and Gene Swanson. Arlene was Marjorie's sister, twelve years her junior. The will had been drawn up prior to Marge's death and Ernie had probably neglected to reread and reevaluate its contents. Logically, the Clarks would have wanted their daughters to be raised by someone who shared their values, was close kin, and whom they believed would put their daughters' needs at a high priority. They had chosen a couple to assure their girls would have surrogate mother *and* father and undoubtedly had discussed this in advance with the Swansons. Yet, having invited his sister and having witnessed a slow return of the family to some semblance of order, Ernie might have named their Aunt Dorothy as legal guardian.

The news was shocking. Having been with the girls for six months, Dorothy was forced to leave. The girls had adjusted well to her; they loved having her around. When she had to return to Cincinnati, Ohio, another tearing of the tenuous family fabric was painful. Sorely frayed emotions flared. "No! We want Dorothy to stay and to be with us! We love her and she loves us!"

But, that was not to be. One more wrenching separation lay directly ahead. "Three months after Dad's death," Julie recalled, "my aunt Dorothy left as my Aunt Arlene and Uncle Gene showed up with their two little sons. The Swansons moved lock, stock, and baggage into the home my father had bought. It was weird to have others come in and take over. Sharon was away at college, so she escaped the impact of the adjustment; but, Judy and I were powerless. We were forced to accept the court's dictates."

Having been out-going and involved in school activities, Julie continued to

Julie, center, was crowned Homecoming Queen

throw herself into her classes. What changed was the intensity with which she stayed out and away from the house as much as possible and, when there, worked on her homework in solitude in her room until late at night. The nightmares of having to quit school and go to work had a beneficial effect of driving an already determined achiever to do even better in her school work. College represented an escape for Sharon and Julie turned her determination toward keeping her grades high. She would qualify for college, be accepted for entrance, and would go on with school. She would manage it *on her own.*

She knew her father and mother would have been completely supportive. But, with the Swansons in charge of the purse strings, Julie had no idea whether there would be any money to help her achieve any goals. Tenaciously, she grasped the idea of going to college like an eagle's talons grasp a fish. It was a lifeline, a promise of better times to come, a means of escape.

Chile, South America

Prior to Ernie's death, Julie and some of her high school friends had applied to spend a semester in foreign study. The applicants underwent reviews of their scholastic records and personal interviews and focused on the use to which a student would later put such a valuable opportunity. Julie was one of a few juniors at

San Carlos High to be chosen. Among her friends, Lisa Geraci was chosen to travel in South America and another went to Mexico.

The first of the siblings to travel abroad, Julie was honored to be selected to study in Chile; yet, she felt overwhelmed by her tragedies. She couldn't imagine having the strength to take on such a challenge so soon. But, Aunt Dorothy and those who had helped her through the agonizing deaths of her mother and father – Katie Couk and Polly Geraci – joined her teachers in urging her to accept this rare chance to extend her envelope, to push past her limits.

The Experiment in International Living, which continues to send students abroad, had existed as an educational program for high school youth for more than seventy years. Under its auspices, Julie was sent to live with a host family. It would mean leaving her sisters behind; but the opportunity was expected to fully immerse her in the culture of Chile and encourage further understanding of global neighbors.

The thought of moving into the home of strangers in a distant country was stimulating; it was also a bit terrifying. All of the recent changes had been so drastic and so dreadful! It was almost beyond her to think of the challenge of learning new language skills, meeting a wide circle of new people, and becoming involved in the myriad of similarities *and* differences of the world.

Brochures painted a rosy picture, "Experimenters focus on themes such as community service, language study, ecology, travel, or the arts, as they enjoy life with their host families and participate in activities with their group."

In reality, Julie would be headed for Santiago, Chile – another world away. On the positive side, she recognized she could escape from the difficulties of adding two little boys and new surrogate parents to her life. She recalled her father saying, "Women. I'm surrounded by women. Even the cats are females." Now, suddenly, two little boys joined the mix …and her mother and father would *never* return.

Julie recalled being seated at the dinner table one evening and, when she reached for a second ear of corn, Arlene slapped her hand. To Julie's amazed look, she said, "We have two growing boys who need that more than you do."

It wasn't a happy household. The strain on everyone was palpable.

Julie gave in to those who urged her to go to South America. The concept was formidable, but she left not long thereafter. A part of her ached for her sisters and the friends with whom she felt safe and comfortable; a part of her was relieved to stay away from the house. It was no longer a home. A foreign country held promise of change and improvement.

During the selection for the international experience, Julie had to discuss plans for doing something with the language studies later in her life. "I had taken the requisite Spanish classes at San Carlos High," she recalled. "I thought I knew the language; but, I *didn't*. Just as in our country dialects differ across the nation, I was going to discover terrific struggles with understanding idiomatic expressions in a rapid, strange tongue.

"When I first arrived, I was placed with a very poor family in the southern part of the country. I had a Chilean 'brother' named Alfonso and I moved into a hovel, little more than four walls with one low door. The parents of the family weren't warm. The sad truth was they couldn't afford another mouth to feed and I was obviously a burden. Not long after I arrived, the mama went outside and I heard a loud squawking. She was twisting the neck off a chicken to put into the pot for dinner. Blood spurted as the chicken dashed crazily in the throes of death. When she served it in soup, it made me literally sick. I couldn't face chicken. I didn't want to *be* there. On top of all I'd been through, I just couldn't *handle* it."

The culture shock was real. "I stayed with the family for three weeks. It became increasingly obvious the family didn't have room for 'la gringa' and I didn't want to stay. Fortunately, the managers of the program found another family for me. This time I was transferred to Antofagasta in the Atacama Desert to live with the Ortiz family in Los Regimentos, a military base."

El Norte Grande, the Atacama Desert

"What a vast improvement for me. This time the Experiment in International Living truly taught me its purpose and served to give me a heightened respect for the Chileans and a renewed enthusiasm for speaking Spanish. I discovered, to my surprise, I suddenly was *dreaming* in Spanish. I didn't have to go through the laborious task of thinking in English and translating word for word to Spanish before speaking or thinking in Spanish and translating the words to English.

"The father of the family was a military officer and he and his wife lived in a large and spacious home, a dramatic contrast to Alfonso's family home. I had a 'sister' Carmen with whom I left for school each morning; she attended El Colegio, the high school, and I went to La Universidad. The credits I earned were directly applicable as college credit. If I was able to go to college, I would major in Spanish and the earned credits would help with that goal."

Antofagasta was beautifully situated in El Norte de Chile. Known as the capital of its region, it presented an interesting contrast of sparse aridity of the mineral-rich Atacama Desierto with the sapphire blue surf of the Pacific Ocean to the west and rugged mountains to the east. It was the site of "The Pacific War of 1879 to 1883," a conflict between Chile, Bolivia, and Peru erupted over the taxation of the lucrative mining of nitrate saltpeter. Chile occupied Antofagasta; Bolivia, allied with Peru, declared war. Defeated decisively by the Chileans, Bolivia withdrew from the conflict in 1881, losing more than the opportunity to harvest nitrate saltpeter. In ceding its Atacama Province to Chile in 1884, Bolivia lost its frontage on the ocean.

Julie especially liked Antofagasta's beautiful beaches like her own in California. She visited Almejas, Huascar, and Balneario Municipal, all located close to La Universidad. Given the chance to ride horses on the beach, she rejoiced. "This was the first

Julie enjoys the red convertible provided for her use as Miss San Carlos 1966

time in my life I'd ridden a horse and I even learned to 'march' a horse. In really *experiencing* the life in another nation, I developed a healthy respect for the Chileans and the values important to them. Simultaneously, I strengthened the intense patriotism I felt – and feel to this day – for my own country, the United States of America. My love of country is very real and I have the Chilean experience to thank for having emphasized the greatness of America our nation's people enjoy."

A Return to California

Because her sister Sharon had set a marriage date, Julie cut short her stay and left Chile after a ten-month stay instead of the expected twelve. The year was 1965 and, although she held mixed feelings about returning to what must have become the Swanson's home instead of her own, she looked forward more eagerly than she would have expected to return to California.

It was good, and important, to be able to participate in Sharon's wedding and she hoped Sharon and John De Vos would be happy. She knew that she'd miss having Sharon come home from college and would miss the comfort Sharon represented.

Miss San Carlos, 1966

However, her relationship with Arlene and Gene hadn't improved. Judy got along with them, but Julie found it tough to live under the same roof. She continued to avoid the house, immersing herself in her senior year at San Carlos High as she had in life in Chile. "I excelled because I worked very hard," she said. "I was a member of the Varsity Pom Pon team and I became involved in gymnastics. I purposely tried to miss a lot of dinners, hoping I'd get home after they had all eaten. I didn't like Arlene and she didn't like me."

Teenaged girls often chafe against the authority figure within even the most loving of homes; Arlene represented the authority and became the target against whom Julie pushed. Conversely, having a beautiful young woman blossom before her very eyes might have been challenging for the woman who had not borne her and lacked the tolerance of maternal ties. A popular, active, and developing beauty might have represented competition.

"There was little about my life that seemed to interest Arlene, although Gene recognized that I was a hard worker," Julie said. "If he passed my room and saw me working on homework, he'd say, 'burning the midnight oil are we?' He was supportive, which I appreciated."

As a Pom Pon girl, Julie attended all the practices and all of the athletic games. A popular student, she dated and enjoyed dances and parties. A beauty, she was honored to be crowned Homecoming Queen as a senior and, after graduation from high school, she was chosen to represent her city as Miss San Carlos in 1966. Her Uncle Gene had encouraged her to compete for Miss San Carlos, helping her receive a nomination. He and Arlene seemed to enjoy that honor in Julie's life.

UC Santa Barbara

Julie applied to and was accepted by the University of California, Santa Barbara. She recalled bringing her notification home and having Arlene ask, "Who's going to pay for this?'

"I didn't know and when I shrugged, she said, 'Well, *we* don't have that kind of money.'"

Still a teenager, she wasn't sophisticated enough to demand, "Was there no money left in my father and mother's estate? Why did Gene find enough money to go to real estate school here in California?"

She didn't know the answers. But, anger sometimes can be a great motivator. She scraped to make college happen. "In addition to having won a monetary award for the Vocational Arts," she said, "I did some research and applied for and received a hardship scholarship from the Bank of America."

While Judy opted to remain in San Carlos, attend the College of San Mateo, and to find a good job, Julie packed her clothes and books and headed for the beautiful coastal city of Santa Barbara. She remembered how her parents had made a big deal of Sharon going off to San Jose State College. They'd packed a trunk, loaded all of Sharon's belongings into the car, and had driven her lovingly toward the next step in her life.

"When *I* left for college, Arlene and Gene put me on a plane and said, 'Your stuff will arrive in a couple of days.' It was so cold. So impersonal. I'm not sure what I expected, but I was both disappointed and relieved to be going away."

College proved to be a turning point in Julie's life. When she returned to San Carlos after her freshman year, she discovered her aunt and uncle had turned her bedroom into a den. "It was awful. All of my personal belongings had been boxed up. I didn't have a room to call my own, a place to go. I was crushed. I barely knew which way to turn."

**Flight offers an entirely different perspective
and lifts a pilot the magical realm
previously claimed by the birds.**

Julie and her Mopar T-34

CHAPTER FIVE: *SEGUE TO THE SEVENTIES*

Julie wondered, *How much more can happen? How much more can I endure? What in the world am I supposed to do?*

She didn't want to stay in Santa Barbara and work during the summers, but what were her options?

Having a twin sister helped to ease the return to the house that was no longer a home. She felt comfortable with Judy. She knew her parents would have welcomed her home and, fortunately, Sharon, still a pillar of strength, made up for the haunting lack of parental affection she had been missing. Sharon even visited Julie in Santa Barbara a few times, giving her much of the caring attention to help Julie cope on her own.

Julie as a college freshman

Santa Barbara

Seeing Pacific Air Lines aircraft taking off and landing at an airport nearby also helped. Jet aircraft had become the norm and Julie wished her father could have lived to have transitioned into them. She knew he had flown the Caravelle once; but, he would have loved jet piloting.

55

One day, with a few extra dollars in her hand left over from some of the money Arlene sent for the purchase of books, Julie rode her bicycle across the Goleta Bridge to Goleta Airfield. She took an introductory ride in a light aircraft, her first flight lesson in a Cessna 150. She tasted the thrill that gave focus to the rest of her life.

Love helped to ease the transition, too. During their senior year, Julie's friend Candy Wilson and her date John Hutley set Julie up on a blind date with Ken Hughes. Afterwards, the four of them double dated often and, in addition to the Senior Prom, Ken and Julie dated steadily throughout 1965 and 1966. Ken held a Private Pilot's certificate and he, too, eased her loneliness, flying to Santa Barbara to see her several times.

It wasn't until later she discovered Ken's dad had flown as an airline pilot with Pacific Air Lines; he and his wife had known Ernie and Marge Clark. The relationship was made even more special.

Julie and Ken were athletic and out-going. Good at waterskiing and snow skiing, the two spent wonderful hours together and, by 1968, were engaged to be married.

The United States of "The Sixties" was a confusion of contrasts. In the year Marjorie died, 1963, Martin Luther King's famous speech at a celebration of the Centennial of the Emancipation Proclamation encouraged a later gathering of hundreds of thousands who marched in support of civil rights. In contrast, the U.S. Supreme Court ruled it unconstitutional to read Bible verses in public schools.

In the year Ernie died, 1964, Congress gave President Lyndon B. Johnson the go-ahead to use all means in opposition to any attack on U.S. forces and aggression by others. In contrast, as tumult and aggression involved U.S. troops in Southeast Asia, citizens on the homefront were seeing Oscars presented in Hollywood to shows as light and benign as *My Fair Lady* and *Mary Poppins*.

In 1965, race riots in Los Angeles' Watts killed 34 and destroyed 200 businesses and North America's worst power failure darkened nine states and part of

Canada for twelve hours. Yet love prevailed; nine months later obstetric wards were doing overtime. In 1967, the revered Dr. Martin Luther King opposed the conflict in Vietnam and 50,000 activists demonstrated at the Pentagon. In contrast, the hot topic of the Congress was Presidential Succession as the 25th Amendment to the Constitution. One year later, students went on strike at Columbia University and at San Francisco College and the use of all artificial methods of birth control was condemned by Pope Paul VI. The Sixties rocked with discontent and rolled with peace and love.

Violence in opposition to the warring in Vietnam and to the "Establishment" seethed throughout college campuses. Ironically, the violence was in opposition to violence and was perpetrated by many of those who sought peace and love. In Santa Barbara, Julie was surrounded by the proponents of "flower power," yet even her benefactor, the Bank of America, suffered being burned. She felt the confusion of the contrasts; she was pulled in both directions. She was a free spirit and a hippie; but, a conscientious objector she was not. When Ken went to Vietnam, she was very supportive. She cared about his safety and the safety of several other friends who served in the controversial fracas that bore all the earmarks of war but was never so declared.

Julie personally mirrored her nation's turmoil of contrasts. She could never deny the patriotism and the appreciation she had long felt for the United States. Yet, as a college student, she was influenced by many of those who were around her. She and Ken learned the highs of marijuana and, in the Vietnam conflict, they discovered the lows of separation. Ken joined the Warrant Officer Program and became a U.S. Army helicopter pilot and Julie traveled to Beeville, Texas, to see Ken pin on his wings. She was there to hold him before he left for Vietnam.

"The agony of the conflict in Southeast Asia ruined a lot of people's lives," she said. A different man returned from the conflict than the lover Julie had known. She flew to Hawaii to meet him during a Rest and Recuperation break (R&R) in his tour of duty. Julie was excited to see him and eagerly looked forward to a wonderful few days. She was disappointed. Ken was withdrawn and quiet, no longer the outgoing, sociable man she had intended to marry. As a rescue helicopter pilot, he had seen the worst. He spoke very little and spent most of their stay simply staring at the ocean. She didn't know how to help him; she couldn't imagine the sights he'd seen, the horror he'd had to face. She didn't know the right things to say. His alienation was shared with many of his military buddies who despaired of reconciling a desire to serve their country with anguish over the management of an unpopular conflict. Their pain was acute.

Later, conservative attorney and legal affairs counsel Ann Coulter wrote, in her best-selling book *Slander*, "Robert McNamara, mastermind of America's defeat in Vietnam, was sniping about [U.S. President George W.] Bush's handling of the Chinese plane crisis. Bush, it seems, had departed from the prized McNamara dispute-resolution technique, which consists of starting a ground war in a jungle, losing the war, condemning millions of people to live under a communist tyranny, and then casually announcing twenty-five years later that [he] knew the war was doomed from the start."

At the microphone encouraging fliers to choose TWA

No wonder their pain was acute.

Do You Want To Travel?

In 1968, Julie had joined the Gamma Beta Chapter of Alpha Phi Sorority and had a wide circle of friends. All during the school year, she relished the comfort of the sorority house, yet despaired that it wouldn't be open during the summer. She easily would have remained in Santa Barbara, worked during the summer, and resumed classes in the fall. As the spring semester wound down and the threat of having nowhere to go loomed, Julie eyed other directions. Bicycling to classes one morning, she passed a sign posted outside of one of the academic buildings at U.C. Santa Barbara. It beckoned, "Do You Want To Travel?" Julie parked her bike and followed up.

Interviews were being held by Trans-World Airlines in an initial phase of hiring hostesses. "The signs were intriguing: 'See the World. Fly with TWA;'" she said. "I didn't talk about this with anyone; I just went in and filled out an application. In order to qualify for the job and to be old enough to serve alcoholic beverages, I was guilty of making one fateful mistake. I put down my birth date as having been 1947 instead of 1948. I went on with school and, for a few months, kind of forgot about it."

When she received the notice inviting her for further interviews, officials of TWA contacted her and offered to send tickets for a flight from Los Angeles to Kansas City. Because of her fluency in a second language, Julie was considered for international flights.

"Not many were chosen for the job," she said. "They were very selective. When we went through our classes, we started off with twenty-five in each class. It seemed girls were washed out if they so much as

"We were stamped out like so many cookie cutter sweets."

looked at somebody wrong. We were lodged in Dos Mundos, a gated apartment community. It not only was closed tightly every night, the gate was electrically charged. No men were allowed. It was very strict, almost like being in jail.

"Training was tough, but it was all about airplanes, which made it more than fun for me. When I was a little girl, if my mother or dad couldn't find me, I'd be perched on a picket fence across the street looking down and watching the airplanes landing and taking off by San Francisco Bay. I was happy to have the chance to *study* about aircraft.

"They judged us as if they wanted a series of little clones. Our height, weight, hairdo, cosmetics, speech, and the fit of our clothes were kept within exacting limits. The training included lessons in poise, in carriage, in conformity, and in matters of etiquette. During the training, we were to be called 'hostesses,' and they were quite strict about it. They instilled in our brains, 'stewards serve pigs.' We wore our wings on our hats; we wore girdles and fake eyelashes and we endured repetitive weight and girdle checks. We all had the same haircut and were made to look like one another; we were stamped out like so many cookie cutter sweets."

Julie also had to pass a very involved test to prove her ability to speak Spanish. But challenges always appealed to her competitive spirit. She aced everything.

Unfortunately, just two days prior to graduation, she was called into the front office. Mr. Braun sat behind his desk holding a ticket. He said, "Do you know what this is?"

Julie answered, "It looks like an airline ticket."

"Right," said Mr. Braun. "It is your ticket to return home."

Julie was floored. *Home?*

"We have discovered a discrepancy between your application and your pass-

Julie, with other Air Hostesses hired by TWA, said, "They wanted a series of little clones."

60

port. Evidently your actual date of birth is later than the date you gave to us. We'll have to send you home."

Julie serves as an Air Hostess

She had sent home for the passport obtained for her trip to Chile and hadn't given a thought to the discrepancy in the dates of birth. The reality of having lied on the application hit her hard. She had so wanted this job. She felt horrified to think she might have to crawl back to the Swansons in disgrace. She immediately recognized the valuable lesson she had learned and she started to cry.

Then Mr. Braun reached forward and opened a drawer in his desk. "However," he said, "your conduct and your academics here have been exemplary. You have won the Training Performance Honors Award for your class." He drew a plaque out of his desk and held it up for her to see. "We've already engraved your name on this award."

Julie looked up at him. He finished with, "we'll not let you go. But we hope this occurrence is never repeated."

A relieved Julie recalled, "Those who graduated were divided into two groups and we nicknamed ourselves the 'Baker's Dozen' and the 'Dirty Dozen.' It was a reminder of my dad's 'Dirty Thirty.'

"I appreciated the Training Performance Honors. I was gratified, too, to be chosen for international flights as only two out of twenty-six were so qualified. I had dashed into the initial interview on a whim, now I was leaving school before having finished at UC-Santa Barbara. Once hired, I knew I was headed for a completely new and different world.

"I went home to San Carlos and casually announced that I was leaving college, I'd been hired by TransWorld Airlines as a hostess, and I was moving to live in New York City. To my aunt and uncle and my sisters, this came out of the blue. They had no inkling I had even applied. I could see the shock on their faces, but there was nothing more to be said except our goodbyes.

"A world away in New York, four of us hostesses roomed together in a 24-story apartment building in Queens. It was the start of a long lasting friendship between Gayle Shurtz Cook, Peggy Bircher Dossi, Judy Pettit Juergens, and I. We called ourselves the 'Hawkers' because we liked checking out good-looking guys, 'Hawks.' Our friendship formed and was to endure.

"I flew with TWA to numerous European destinations, but used my language skills primarily when we flew in and out of Spain and Portugal."

Beauty Matters

After a year-and-a-half with TWA, an accident brought the job to an end. During a vacation, Ken Hughes returned from his tour of duty in Vietnam and the two drove to get their hands on a pair of water skis for an afternoon of fun. As they rounded a corner, Ken's German shepherd, who had been in the back seat of his Karmann Ghia, jumped into the front. Ken wrestled to shove the dog back and he lost control of the car. The little car plowed into a tree. Ken was banged up and Julie was thrown through the windshield. Glass shards raked across her face.

The first flight hostesses had been required to be nurses, a rule eased by the time of Julie's hire. But flight hostesses of the 1960s were hired on the basis of good looks. For Julie, the wound and the scarring brought her job to an end. She was grounded.

Forty-four stitches were needed to repair the scarring wound across her upper face and down to her eyebrows. She wore an eye patch until the danger of infection was minimal. Even worse, her first surgical operation resulted in keloid tissue, a growth of fibroblastic tissue exacerbated the wound.

When she overheard doctors mentioning the idea of plastic surgery, she rebelled, "I don't want plastic surgery. Sew it up. Just stitch it up."

The second surgical procedure was a form of abrasion—a scraping of the ridge formed along the scar. Julie wore a patch on her face for months.

Grounded from flying, Julie was free to visit Ken Hughes at his new assignment as a helicopter instructor at Fort Rucker, Alabama. She flew to Enterprise, Alabama and laughed to

Learning to fly a Cessna-150

see the town's statue, a Monument to the Boll Weevil. The sign welcoming travelers to Enterprise stated, "Home of the Boll Weevil Monument, Where Cotton Used to be King" and referred to the loss of the economic base due to the pest so destructive of the important cotton crops of the past. Having to change their agricultural base to raising peanuts turned out to be lucky for the farmers of Enterprise. The monument, which was created in Italy in 1917 and originally dedicated in 1919, represented the debt owed to the pest. The boll weevil, through destruction, created an awareness of the value and success of crop diversity.

In Enterprise, Julie got involved teaching gymnastics. Enterprise Junior High School's building had been burned and school officials maintained classes in portable metal buildings belonging to Fort Rucker. Julie was hired to replace a teacher who had been injured. She said, "I didn't have teaching credentials. I was amazed I could be hired without a degree and the necessary papers. But, although I enjoyed teaching Spanish to the kids, I came home exhausted at night. I developed a deep appreciation for teachers and the jobs they do. Teaching school was *not* where I wanted to be. Not at all."

She and Ken decided marriage was not where they wanted to be, either. Just as it had on millions of others, the Vietnam conflict had taken its toll on Ken. So many men had faced battles they found difficult to support when surrounded with the in-your-face anti-war demonstrators at home. Both Julie and Ken had matured and changed. Both were introduced to other paths to follow, other careers to pursue. Tragically, Ken was in a devastating motorcycle accident after his return to California. Julie cared deeply for him and hated to know he'd been badly hurt in his accident.

"He was riding across the San Mateo Bridge carrying a set of golf clubs on the cycle with him. He was headed for a golf game in Menlo Park with his dad, Bill Hughes, and a pickup driver rear-ended him. The guy claimed he never even saw Ken. The force of the crash threw Ken into the back of a huge 18-wheeler."

Ken spent a long time in the hospital and in recuperation. Julie, whose wounds had transferred her from being a flight attendant stationed out of New York City to being a ground hostess at San Francisco Airport, saw him often. But their relationship was not to be.

She said, "When he heard I was taking flying lessons in Santa Barbara, he had been completely supportive. He thought my interest in flying was just great, especially when he saw I had to do it all on my own. Ken was truly my first love. Our breakup really broke my heart."

To Fly

Julie appreciated TWA's ground hostessing job, but hated the work. It failed miserably in comparison with winging her way between the bright lights and glitter of the Big Apple to the compelling and interesting capitals of Europe. What she really wanted to do was to follow her father's love of the sky. She wanted to *fly*.

She now knew there was money in the Clark estate. She also knew, had her father been alive, he would have supported her every step of the way. When she approached Arlene for money for flying lessons, she asked, "Could you help me? Or, could we work something out?"

Julie remembered hearing Arlene say, "Your dad was *killed* in a plane crash! Why in the hell would you ever want to fly?"

"My dad was dead before the plane hit the ground," Julie said. "My dad was *murdered!* His death had *nothing* to do with a plane crash. I want to learn to fly. I flew with my dad a lot when I was a little girl. Flying has been on my mind ever since."

Told, "Well, we're not going to help you with flying lessons. If flying is something you want to do, you're on your own."

Julie had survived worse conversations. She had learned persistence and dedication from *much* more tragic circumstances than being refused by an aunt. Yet, the refusal galvanized her into action. Julie changed from simply wanting to fly to becoming determined to demonstrate just how far she could go on her own, just how much she could accomplish. Her dad was with her in spirit and she felt surer of herself than she had ever felt before. She was *going* to fly!

**As popular a performer in Canada as in the United States,
Julie's air show performance
is seen and enjoyed by
thousands of people annually.**

Julie with her Mopar T-34

CHAPTER SIX: HER WINGS, HER SKY

**Julie is out in front,
Marine World Africa USA**

Nothing was going to stop her now! Oh, the marvelous trips she had taken with her father. Special moments passed like a slide show of images in her mind's eye. She recalled begging him to take her along, which he often did when his flight was going to be an out and back. She could feel his hands lifting her as a tiny child, helping her up into the airliner, strapping her into a seat, and patting her head as he smiled his unforgettable smile. Sometimes he sneaked her up into the cargo hold, telling her, 'You stay right there. I'll come to get you.' He'd climb aboard and retrieve her, taking her forward to a seat and fastening a seat belt around her.

Her baby book noted she'd taken her very first trip with her Dad and Mom when she was just three months old. Although she had no recollection of that particular Douglas DC-3 flight, she just knew she had *always* loved flying.

"I never had enough money," she admitted. "When I was attending school at UC-Santa Barbara, I could barely scrape up enough money for one flight lesson. I'd ride my bike across the freeway to Goleta Airport and cherish the one flight my money would buy. Then several weeks passed before I could afford it again.

"I guess it was a good thing Arlene didn't pay much attention to my time at college. I managed to squeak extra dollars by asking for money for school books. I kept thinking she would ask, 'How many courses are you taking?' 'How many credits are allowed each semester?' I used every spare bit of change for flying lessons. I got my Student Pilot certificate and Class III medical and, on 14 April 1969, I soloed. A first solo is a day you never forget. The certificate almost burned a hole in my wallet; I was eager to get on with training. I loved it from the start.

"But bitterness burned, too. I kept thinking, 'If my Dad was alive, he would have been right in there with everything I did. I really resented it so much."

Before she could solo, Julie's decision to leave school and go to work with TWA ended flight lessons in Santa Barbara. In New York opportunities to fly commercial airliners to Europe abounded, but chances to fly private aircraft, for someone without a car who had to rely on public transportation, were severely limited. Then, having returned to California to endure the surgeries to repair her facial lacerations, she had been forced, at least until her injuries healed, to push flight training into her future.

Flying was alluring, intoxicating. Like a remote star in the farthest galaxy, it shone as a tantalizing goal, beckoning, yet remaining beyond reach.

If ground hostessing for TWA had been more rewarding, she might have filled the coffers a bit more quickly. It was nothing like the magic of her earlier flights to Spain, Portugal, and other cities in Europe; but the lack of excitement was partially compensated by the steady salary. She might have held on to the job, had airline passengers all fallen into the category of jocular, pleasant clients; but, one particular confrontation soured her interest in the job.

Julie, monitoring Gate 22, was still bruised and wearing the patch over her face, but her spirit hadn't been dampened.

He walked up and asked curtly, "Flight 100. Washington, DC. What gate?" and she coyly glanced at the Solari Boards displaying announcements of arrivals and departures overhead.

She teased, trying to be funny, "I see Gate 22. What do you see?"

The man snarled, "Young lady, you give me another smart remark and I'll give you another scar to think about."

The traveling public could be charming. As this man attested, it could also be fraught with the surly, the sarcastic, the critical, and the complaining. Julie recognized it was the *job* she didn't like. It was time for a change.

Another Love

Rick Ames

The phone rang one day and Rick Ames was on the line. "When he said his name," Julie said, "all I could think was, 'Ricky Ames?' I'd known Rick from my grade school days. He lived kitty-corner from our home and I often saw him in the neighborhood. Sometimes we met in the street and he talked about his ROTC training; I told him about wishing to take flying lessons. I'd known Rick had gone to San Jose State College after we'd graduated from high school, but I was surprised to hear from him. We used to go on church ski groups together up to Lake Tahoe and during my junior and senior years of high school I dated his best friend, Dave Cranfield. Now, Rick was asking me for a date! I looked forward to seeing him."

Little did Julie know how much she and Rick Ames would have in common. Little did she dream that she was planning a first date with the man whom she would marry.

Survival

To find a place to live and to find lucrative jobs to pay for room and board *and* some extra money for flight lessons consumed Julie. She not only found one job, she took on several. During 1972, 1973, and 1974, she balanced an exhausting

**For two years, Julie performed at
Marine World Africa USA**

schedule. She was hired as a cocktail waitress at the lounge of Charlie Brown's Steakhouse south of San Francisco, started performing daily in the waterski show at Marine World, and followed her first airline job, flight attending for TWA, with a third job as a purser with San Francisco and Oakland Helicopter Airlines (SFO), and a fourth as a flight attendant for World Airways, a non-scheduled (non-sched) line. She said, "You meet people who have no idea what it means to set goals requiring so much time, effort, and expense. They don't know what hard work is all about. On the other hand, they miss the thrill of achievement and the pleasure of coming into contact with the great people who help you along the way."

With SFO Helicopter Airlines, Julie stepped back in time almost as if she'd returned to the glory days of barnstorming. Hired to sell tickets to passengers for commuter flights between Oakland, Berkeley, Marin, and San Francisco, she spent special hours with professional helicopter pilots whirling in sightseeing flights over beautiful San Francisco Bay. As purser, she handled the tickets and helped passengers into the craft. She climbed aboard, flew with them, helped them deplane, and then turned to start ticketing a whole new set of customers.

"When no passengers were aboard, the pilots John Chesley and Chris Miller gave me stick time," she said. "Sometimes we flew empty up to the helicopter landing pad out near Berkeley, took on and flew the commuting public, and then returned empty. I cherished those chances to handle the controls. I only worked for them for about six months; but I was busy, out on the ramp, around aircraft and other people. I really enjoyed it, I enjoyed John and Chris. It was a great job. Sometimes John would dip down over Charlie Brown's and shine his landing light in through the lounge windows. I knew he was signaling; he'd be landing at Oakland and arriving at Charlie Brown's in about an hour."

SFO Helicopter Airlines owed its origin to the success of Sikorsky's S-62, the company's first amphibious helicopter. With so much overwater flying required, engineers at the Connecticut Sikorsky plant re-engined the S-55, adding the General Electric T-58 gas-turbine and floats. Originally, SFO Helicopter Airlines

As part of her job with SFO, San Francisco and Oakland Helicopter Airlines, Julie modeled for magazine advertisements

leased two S-62s and then purchased three more. Because the airline required no subsidized funding, SFO received the first permanent C.A.B. (Civil Aeronautics Board) certificate to be awarded any helicopter carrier.

"I loved helicopter flying," Julie said. "If I could have figured out a use for it, I would have pursued a rotary-wing rating. Without being able to envision a job, I couldn't justify the expense.

She loved waterskiing, too. Having learned to waterski while she and Ken Hughes were in Alabama, Julie tried out for a job she saw advertised.

Wanted: Professional Waterskiers. Must be able to perform. Marine World Africa USA.

"I could do that," she decided. "It sounds like fun." As she tried-out, she appreciated the Army wife at Fort Rucker who taught her fancy waterski moves.

Julie's audition put her onto the water immediately. Towed behind a camera boat, she was told to demonstrate some specific waterski moves – crossing the wake, single ski reverses, using toe holds, and foot and hand position changes. When they asked her to form a pyramid, she followed their instructions, grateful for her gymnastic agility.

"Even though I had been feeling as if I was coming down with the flu, I scrambled up onto the shoulders of two guys fairly easily," She said. "I went into the office at the end of the try-outs, feeling even sicker to my stomach and, as the manager welcomed me, telling me when to come to work, I suddenly felt feverish and sweaty. I was going to throw up! I turned to find the only container available. The interview ended as I embarrassed myself by throwing up directly into his trash basket. Fortunately, he didn't renege on hiring me. I started work as soon as I could shake the flu."

Eventually, Julie topped a group of nine skiers and became an important addition to the cast. She performed with the waterski show at Marine World Africa USA for two and a half years.

But, waterskiing wasn't all thrilling and glamorous. Ski shows were scheduled daily, rain or shine, and translated to three shows per day in the summer and two shows during the winter. Each day started with the troupe washing the boats: a camera boat, a boat for trick skiing, a power boat for pulling the pyramids, a boat for waterski jumps, and back up boats. In between shows, they wound ropes, varnished the docks, painted, made costumes, and did whatever the managers required of them.

"It was a weird, clandestine group – almost a carnival of characters involved," Julie said. "A married couple ran the water show with tight, iron fists. You had better not be just standing around and, if you were winding a ski rope, you'd better be doing it *correctly*. If not, the wife grabbed it, threw it, and said, 'Get it right!'

"We all did the marijuana bit there; but I didn't like to smoke. I did reluctantly eat some of the laced brownies shared by the cast members.

"When I was hired, I wasn't surprised they wanted to see what you looked like

72

in a bathing suit. Like a Miss San Carlos competition and the hostessing for TWA, this was show business and looks mattered. But, if you were changing your costume and the boss walked in, he might say, 'Just a minute. I want to see you naked. Show me what you look like.' He was in charge. You did as you were told. He never made any advances, but I learned I had better not try to cover up. Those in charge wanted what they wanted."

Although they were dating whenever possible, Rick Ames spent much of 1973 and 1974 away. Rick had joined the U.S. Navy and was assigned to pilot training in Pensacola, Florida. There he earned the gold wings of a Navy pilot and thereafter was shipped off on requisite Naval cruises. Julie wrote letters to him, telling of some of the weird demands she was getting. She knew there was nothing he could do, but she wanted to share some of the things she was enduring and what it meant to her to make enough money to be able to fly. She never lost sight of her goal. She let nothing stand in her way!

Having a job starting at one in the afternoon and only lasting about four or five hours – and *paid well* – meant she could take flying lessons each morning and moonlight as a cocktail waitress each night. It was too lucrative to pass up.

Foster City

Her Uncle Gene, now heavily involved in real estate, helped her finance the purchase of her first home. He applied what would have been his commission as a down payment on a $35,000 townhouse for her at 1117 Polynesia Drive, Foster City. His donation of $1,700 helped her finance the townhouse at $134 per month and gave her independence for future real estate dealings. The sale of the Foster City condo, for example, resulted in the money to buy a house when she and Rick were married. "I have to thank my uncle for this. Through equity and having established credit, I was able to use each home as a stepping-stone for the subsequent purchase. Gene instilled in me the uselessness of throwing good money down the drain through renting."

Julie's home was south of the San Francisco Airport and close to Redwood

City, where Marine World Africa USA was located. It has since grown into a vast amusement park – Six Flags Marine World – and has been relocated to Vallejo. For Julie, Foster City was the hub of her busy schedule; she lived out of the townhouse and spent all of her time juggling flying lessons, water-skiing, cocktail waitressing, and working with the helicopter and fixed wing airlines.

In the evenings, Julie arrived home from Marine World at 6 p.m., her waist-long hair wet, her eyes stinging from the salt water. After a quick shower, she clipped on a fake hairpiece, smoothed color on her lips, and dashed to Charlie Brown's Steakhouse. In an entirely different role, she served cocktails each evening in Charlie Brown's lounge from 7 o'clock to 2 in the morning. Early most mornings she could be found at the airport. Hers was a wild schedule; she set an exhausting pace.

Interestingly, the regular clients who crowded into her

Julie learned to fly in the popular civilian trainer, the Cessna 150

tables at night were workers at the San Francisco Airport. "I will never forget those guys," she said. "The restaurant was fairly close to the airport and right on the freeway. All of the men who were involved in aviation themselves were supportive when they found out why I was working. I told them about taking flight lessons at San Carlos Airport and they really cheered me on. They gave me great tips.

"They'd come to watch the show at Marine World, then come to Charlie Brown's to tell me all about having seen it. Like John Chesley, all were warm and friendly, a great support group. They recognized hard work and tipped well. They were great to me."

Most importantly, Julie was flying. Her Dad would have been so proud! She passed the written test for Private Pilot and took her flight test in October 1974, becoming a licensed pilot. The more she worked and the more she flew, the more determined she became. She had never tasted a greater thrill of success, had never worked harder to see each subsequent hour posted in her log books.

The Universal World

Having been trained and experienced as a hostess with TWA, Julie was hired easily as a Flight Attendant with Universal Airlines; but the job was short-lived. In 1969, when Julie had launched into her flight training toward her Private Pilot certificate, Universal had a fleet of fifty aircraft – Boeing 727s, Douglas DC-4s and DC-8s, some Lockheed Electras, and others. It was a non-sched airline, as was World, which boasted nine Boeing 707s and four Boeing 727s – a fleet of thirteen – at the same time. It is an intriguing fact of airline management and the vagaries of domestic versus international traffic growth that Universal went out of business and World continued to thrive. The U.S. Court of Appeals for the District of Columbia, the U.S. Supreme Court, and members of Congress and the Administration decided in 1968 that Supplemental Air Carriers could be awarded international *and* domestic routes by the C.A.B., which gave the carriers the opportunity to compete with scheduled carriers for international tours and other business contracts.

Julie was hired and put through training as a flight attendant with Universal World Saturn Overseas National Airways (ONA), which was based out of Oakland. She was in training in 1973 when the airline went under.

She said, "I flew one trip with them, period. We landed in Belgium and, when bankruptcy was announced, the DC-8 on which we'd arrived was immediately impounded. The crew and I came out to get aboard and people were crawling all over the cockpit, stripping it of its airspeed indicators, altimeters, radios, and other gauges. When we asked what they were doing, they told us, 'This plane is going nowhere. It's been grounded.'

"Authorities had asked the pilots for credit cards when we arrived. We wondered at the time, 'What kind of outfit are we working for?' The people stripping the gauges represented a collection agency taking the airplane over.

"It was more than interesting. I had trouble finding a way to fly back to the United States. As an employee, I had the authority to jump on any airline accepting of a Universal crewmember. I had to plead to grab a ride."

The experience of having flown with TWA and Universal placed her in an enviable position to be hired by her next carrier, World Airways, a non-sched operating only three months out of the year. She was hired quickly. They told her the "airline would be glad to have her; when could she start?"

World Airways

While flying for World, Julie accumulated the money necessary to obtain her advanced flight ratings – instrument, commercial, and Certificated Flight Instructor (CFI). Advanced ratings were essential and costly and the quest for more flying time always equated a quest for more money.

Julie started the lucrative business, "Jule's Clocks." Because World obtained its

**Julie and Rick Ames
were married, May 1975**

credentials to fly internationally and became based at Yokota Air Force Base in Yokota, Japan, Julie was sent to live there for 90 days. She explained, "We flew what they called the 'Stars and Stripes Flights.' Under a charter, we carried U.S. military G.I.s to Vietnam, to Hawaii, and to other places for their brief chances at 'R&R.'

"I flew into Korea on one such trip and met a guy who was selling antique wall clocks. I've always loved antiques, so I first was interested in buying a clock of my own. It didn't take long to realize I could buy a clock for $10, could carry it back to the States, and sell it for between $90 to $120. I loved the clocks and loved sharing them with others who loved antiques and hand-made décor like I did. I was thrilled to have found something pleasing to me and pleasing to everyone else who bought one from me. I learned to repair any unexpected damages to glass or wooden parts that resulted during transit; I even learned to repair some of the mechanisms. I earned enough money to pay for a couple of my flight ratings with cash. Having known how hard it was for me to produce the money necessary to keep flying, people who knew me well thought I had robbed a bank."

Trouble could have loomed from authorities. Julie never applied for an import license and she hadn't declared herself as a business. She was focused on furthering her career and was highly motivated. At the start, she did what many travelers do – purchased something for her own use and then found someone who wanted to own it more than she. However, by the time she had purchased two lots of 100 clocks each, she opted to quit before she found herself in hot water.

But, the entrepreneurial spirit has been part and parcel of Julie's life. Without wavering from her goal of becoming a capable and well-paid woman pilot, she explored ventures that proved profitable and established herself as a successful businesswoman.

While flying with World Airways, Julie made friends with other flight attendants and she and Rick Ames grew from having occasional dates to dating seriously. They both enjoyed snow skiing and found several of World's flight attendants who liked to ski, too. One of their greatest joys was to chip in for the rental of a lightplane and then fly to Tahoe to share the cost of a ski cabin while Julie logged the precious hours of flight experience. She said, "Rick thought it was wonderful I had so many 'stewardess buddies' and we could take off for Tahoe and fly back in time for work on Monday. This was really when we grew to be more serious about one another."

No natural beauty on earth surpasses the unbelievable grandeur of the snow-covered High Sierra Mountains with their reflections in the waters of majestic Lake Tahoe. Squaw Valley Ski Resort, a jewel in an alpine valley beneath six visible and crystalline peaks, was a compelling reason for an idyllic weekend and was more than enough to ignite romance. Riding the cable car high into the mountains and sliding off into a pristine world took a skier's breath with its exhilarating cold and for its sublime majesty; each ski weekend was a precious gift. Julie and Rick fell in love – with skiing, with flying, with life, and with one another. They started to plan their wedding.

New Horizons

Julie and Rick Ames rented a Beech Sundowner to fly off on their honeymoon on 10 May 1975. After flying first to San Carlos and then on to San Francisco, they jumped on a Hughes Airwest flight to Puerto Vallarta, Mexico. Not long after, the newly-weds set their sights on Naval Air Station (NAS) Lemoore where Rick was assigned as an A-7 Corsair pilot. A whole new world was opening before Julie Clark Ames. Brochures made Lemoore sound idyllic:

> *In the summer months, Lemoore is hot and dry with cloudless skies. The temperature often rises above 100 degrees; however, humidity usually stays at or below 25 percent. Fog starts to roll in during November through the winter months and usually burns off by the afternoon to yield sunny skies. Beaches are within a two-hour's drive and mountain skiing is less than a three hour's drive.*

By 21 May she and Rick had moved from Foster City. Soon she would be involved with the great fun of making a house into a home. Her flying would take on a whole new dimension with Navy Lemoore and Navy military planes. She wasn't quite through with "Jule's Clocks" and she was about to learn the meaning of the word *Warbird* .

CHAPTER SEVEN: *TALLYING THE HOURS*

The move to Lemoore took Julie forty miles south of Fresno and magical miles into her own future. Not only had the geography changed from the cool, water-drenched influence of the coastal mountains and San Francisco Bay into the sunny and fertile San Joaquin Valley; but the cold, relentless hassle of having to provide for herself was exchanged with a warm, shared closeness of marriage. Julie had done well for herself and now she was a wife, with a fighter pilot husband to consider and love. For his part, Rick was returning from his cruise just as the Vietnam conflict was grinding to a close. Little compared to flying an A-7 Corsair II, an aircraft built for close air support as well as search, surveillance, and attack missions, to and from an aircraft carrier, but he relished being based on solid ground.

Julie threw her considerable energies from balancing three and four jobs into the more focused effort of settling into a new home in Lemoore and finding something lucrative and rewarding in the San Joaquin. When Rick introduced her to civilian flying on Naval Air Station (NAS) Lemoore and gave her a glimpse of the T-34 aircraft available at the Aero Club for her to fly, she was enthralled.

Fly Navy

"I could scarcely believe my good fortune – getting a chance to fly in the single-engine Beech aircraft that were the springboard to flight for so many military pilots! Flying T-34s in 1975 and 1976 at Lemoore was my introduction to a host of things and I had Rick to thank for the opportunities. In the Navy way, I learned to fly formation – learned how to fly on a lead pilot's wing, to hold steady

**Julie and Diane Mann,
at the start of the AWTAR**

and, eventually, to close in tightly and follow the leader. I was taught aerobatics. I'd been shown rolls and loops by some of my instructors, but this was precise aerobatics and a challenge to do well. Then, too, I was trained in tactical maneuvers. My role at Navy Lemoore was to fly with pilots who wanted currency in the single-engine Mentor and I spent almost all of my flight time in one or another of the two T-34B models belonging to the Aero Club."

The T-34 Mentor was designed under the guidance of the famed Walter Beech, who began his illustrious career as an Army aviator in 1917 and in aircraft manufacture with the Swallow Airplane Company in Wichita, Kansas, touted as the "Air Capital of the World." In alliance with Clyde Cessna, they launched the

**An air race crew and
an air race airplane are ready**

Travel Air Manufacturing Company in 1924. This later merged with the Curtiss-Wright Airplane Company of which Beech became president. Striking out on his own, he and his wife, the noted Olive Ann Beech, co-founded Beech Aircraft Company in 1932. During World War II, the company devoted its entire production line to defense and produced more than 7,400 airplanes.

Basing his T-34 design on his Beechcraft Model 35 Bonanza, Walter Beech considered it to be an alternative to North American's AT-6/SNJ; he produced it privately. With renowned test pilot Vern Carstens demonstrating its maneuverability, the T-34 made its debut on 2 December 1948. In part, Carstens had earned his stellar reputation as the pilot who flew the Sikorsky S-38 and S-39 flying boats in Africa and Borneo with famed photographers and explorers Martin and Osa Johnson of Chanute, Kansas. His demonstration impressed the United States Air Force, which placed an

Julie monitors weather reports prior to the AWTAR

order for three aircraft designated as the YT-34. The craft was designed originally with a V-tail, but the production model differed from the Bonanza and bore a conventional tail. The Mentor was demonstrated by famed aerobatic pilots Beverly "Bevo" Howard and Betty Skelton at the 1949 Cleveland Air Races. Walter Beech strongly believed in the capability of his Mentor as a military trainer, but he regrettably died of a heart attack in 1950. It would have pleased Beech to know his design, though it faced stiff competition from the YT 35 Buckaroo, beat the competition for the military contract and went into service with the United States Air Force as the T-34A in 1953 and with the U.S. Navy training fleet as the T-34B in 1955. T-34As were licensed to be built in Canada, Japan, and Argentina and production ran from 1953 to 1956. It was a great craft for a

World Airways helped with sponsorship for the AWTAR

young woman to get her hands on and Julie spent every spare hour logging flight hours and gaining in experience.

Air Racing

Believing an aircraft leased back to the Navy Aero Club could pay for itself

Getting the charts in order for the route of flight

over time, Julie bought a single-engine Rockwell Commander 112A, registration number N1159J, as an investment. When she read of the annual All Women's Transcontinental Air Race (AWTAR), sponsored by The Ninety-Nines, the International Organization of Women Pilots, scheduled for the summer in 1976, she polished the Commander and responded to the call. Pilots are nothing if they are not competitive and up for a challenge. She

entered the race with 59 Juliet and was introduced to a co-pilot to share the expenses and what she hoped would be fun. Getting to actually air race reminded her of the times in the past when her dad had taken her to the San Carlos Airport to see women air racers fly through. She looked forward to trying it herself.

Between 9 and 11 July 1976, Julie teamed with Nebraskan Diane Mann to fly what has popularly been called the Powder Puff Derby, having been given the sobriquet in 1929 by none other than Will Rogers. She was helped, in part, with sponsorship money by World Airways and, pasting a Number 29 on the tail of the Commander, she and Diane departed from Sacramento for the long cross country air race to Wilmington, Delaware. Julie wrote in her logbook, in typical aviation shorthand:

> *Fly by March AFB, very poor vis RAL, thundershowers over Mojave,*
> *5500 feet density altitudes. Wait in SAF for IFR weather in LBB. Max*
> *thunderstorms and rain showers between SAF and LBB. Good fly by in*

The Clark Family: Marjorie and Ernie
with their daughters,
Sharon, Julie, and Judy

Ernie, a Captain for Pacific Air Lines,
piloted the F-27 Friendship.
Pacific Air Lines became Air West
and then Hughes Airwest,
"Top Banana of the West."

Julie, a Pom Pon girl at
San Carlos High School and
Homecoming Queen,
is named
"Miss San Carlos, 1966."

Julie begins her aviation career
as an Air Hostess with TWA, 1968.

Julie and her sister Sharon Clark De Vos.

Fluent in Spanish, Julie flies to
Spain, Portugal, and Mexico.

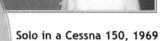

Solo in a Cessna 150, 1969

Practice Makes Perfect for
Marine World Africa USA
1972-1974

Julie marries Rick Ames in May 1975

Their Honeymoon Express is a rented Beech Sundowner

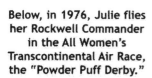

Below, in 1976, Julie flies her Rockwell Commander in the All Women's Transcontinental Air Race, the "Powder Puff Derby."

Hired as a First Officer by
Golden West (the 1st and
only woman pilot),
Julie's airline career
begins in 1977.

Also in 1977, she flies the sister-ship
to her
Dad's F-27
in her Dad's airline,
Hughes Airwest.

On her
days off,
she flies
aerobatics
in a
nimble
Pitts.

Bought sight unseen in
1977, Julie
ferries her
USAF surplus T-34A
from
Alaska to California.

Her restoration project starts
and, painstakingly,
an award-winning
air show airplane results.

A merger takes Julie from Hughes Airwest
to Republic Airlines in 1980.
Another merger takes Republic to Northwest
Airlines in January, 1986.

A Republic Convair 580 flies
"Herman" the duck on the tail.

A merger drops the Republic logo,
"Herman,"
his "tombstone" cites,
He Flied
He Tried
My How
He Tried
Along Came
Northwest
O My How He Died

Below: Julie becomes a Captain, 1983
and the Mopar T-34 soars!

American Aerobatics incorporates
in the late 1980s
Julie displays her
14-carat gold edition Victor engine,
and joins her long-time crew,
Judy and Ron McLane.

She's a
cover girl on
*World Airshow
News.*

Below is her
new Mopar logo.

Misti Flaspohler, her assistant,
fellow pilot, and friend, joins Julie

In the
Canine Corner
is:
left, Mags;

above,
Mollie;

and
right,
Bernie.

SCCA Pro Racing

27 May 1996,
Julie races in the
Dodge Neon Celebrity Challenge

Learning the techniques at the
Dodge Skip Barber Driving School,

she trains in the blue car,
(below),
and earns a
Pro Racing Driver License.

She races in the Grand Prix at
Limerock Park, Connecticut
Drivers in yellow Neons,
like Julie,
are the
Celebrity Drivers

Special Memories for Julie:

Clockwise:
In front of the Mopar trailer
with pioneer aviatrix Bobbi Trout,

with Mike Van Wagenen,

with Gary Loundagin
in front of her home and hangar,

with two "Moms,"
Iris Taggart and Gladys Hood,

at a reunion in 1998 with Air Hostesses
from TWA days - "The Hawkers"
Peggy Bircher Dossi,
Judy Pettit Juergens and
Gayle Shurtz Cook,

and with Tony Olivera.

Julie's home is on
a residential airpark.
A runway is directly
outside of her door.

**Mastering Two Careers:
Northwest Airlines
and the
Mopar T-34**

Below right, Julie and her twin, Judy Grilli

Photo, David Poleski

The painting below is "The Old Work Horse Coming Home," by renowned artist Paul Rendel, ASAA. The DC-9 approaches Minneapolis/St. Paul, a sight familiar to Julie. She logged 13,000 hours in the DC-9!

Wheels for Julie's Mopar Ground Crew

To the right: a portrait of a beauty.

Julie, an award winner,
is honored with:

Flying in the Shrike Commander
with legendary Bob Hoover,

Dancing with Tennessee Ernie Ford
who announced her air show act,

Performing her
aerial ballet to Lee
Greenwood's
"God Bless the U.S.A."

Flying with Robin Leach,

and enjoying the friendship of
Patty Wagstaff,
with their
Green Cheeked Conures
"Buddha" and "Ernie"

With Ninety-Nines
Janie Postlethwaite,
Janet Green,
and
Thon Griffith,
Julie accepts
one of her honors:
"Woman Pilot of
the Year,"
1980.

From Wayne Handley and Judy Scholl,
ICAS 1998, Julie receives the coveted
Art Scholl Memorial Award for Showmanship.

In 2002 she is inducted into
Women in Aviation,
International
Pioneer Hall of Fame.

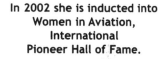

With her at the
Women in Aviation Conference
is Doris Lockness,
her sister Sharon De Vos, (above right)
and "Bravo," Allan Thomas.

WARBIRDS TAKE TO THE AIR

Julie adds her bright T-28
to her hangar and,
as she named the T-34
"Wally" and "Free Spirit,"
she named the T-28
"Top Banana"
in honor of
Hughes Airwest,
"Top Banana of the West."

She flies in the T-28 to the
left, with Mags, and also

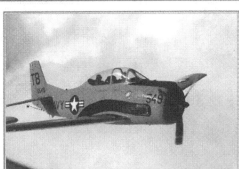

In formation,

She lands in formation
in her T-34
at EAA AirVenture,
Oshkosh, Wisconsin,

and on the tarmac, she shares a
moment with Allan Thomas

and takes to "Top Banana."

Julie flies "Left Wing" to Lead
T-28 Formation Flight at
EAA AirVenture,
Oshkosh, Wisconsin

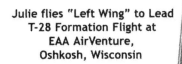

Lifts Off

Flies her Mopar T-34 straight
toward the camera

and

Enjoys one of two
unforgettable
chances
to fly the
air show routine
of the
CAF Aerial
Demonstration Team,
The Snowbirds
1995

A Final Flight and A Retirement Party
9 and 15 October 2003
With her twin, Judy Grilli;
Rick Toscano, Northwest Airlines;
Rick Berecz, Mopar;
Bob Donnell, her dad's good friend;
and VIPs: Judy Grilli, Gladys Hood,
Sharon De Vos, Allan Thomas, and Iris Taggart.
Below right, Larry Littlepage and Emma.

Congratulations, Julie!

In a memorable moment, Julie's A 320 receives a
celebratory Water Salute from
the fire engine crews, Sacramento.
Retirement from Northwest Airlines gives Julie more
time for her air show career, for mentoring others,
and for the rest of her life.

OKC, met by Rockwell Commander dealer. Over flew Little Rock (LIT) and landed at Nashville (BNA), warm greeting. Very high winds at PKB, long delay prior to TO. Very poor vis over the Allegheny Mountains, Great reception in Wilmington, Del. Score over all was +13. Total flying time: 20.6 hours. Diane Mann copilot, TAR #29.

To decode: The flight departed Sacramento, overflew March Air Force Base, then proceeded to Riverside, California (RAL); to Santa Fe, New Mexico (SAF); to Lubbock, Texas (LBB); to Oklahoma City, Oklahoma (OKC); to Little Rock, Arkansas (LIT); to Nashville, Tennessee (BNA); to Parkersburg, West Virginia (PKB); and to a terminus in Wilmington, Delaware.

Checking the oil quantity level

The skies were turbulent in some areas and a smoldering storm brewed within the cockpit as well. Angered that early in the flight she and her co-pilot had wandered off course, found themselves over the Salton Sea, and lost some time with a navigational mistake, a short spat grew in intensity as did the tension of the race. Julie and Diane were barely speaking by the time they arrived in Wilmington. "I remember saying, 'The Salton *Sea!* Diane, we are so far *off!*'" said Julie. "But, in fairness, she only had 80 hours of flying time. It was depressing, though, to screw up right at the *start*. But, despite the gaffe, we finished 92 out of 200. I mean, we finished in the top half. Unfortunately, we didn't finish up as friends.

"Her husband, Bob Mann, with whom I have remained friendly to date, had a wood-working company. He generously helped to finance the flight. We also owed thanks to World Airways and my Uncle Gene, who again came to my rescue. Rather than share the cockpit for a return to California, Diane opted to fly home via a commercial airliner. The competitive spirit is alive and well in air racing. Their struggles were no different than many such arguments born of preparation, navigation, timing, communication, weather briefings, flight planning, and the angst racing can engender. They weren't the first duo – nor were they the last – to find it difficult to share a cockpit.

On 16 July 1976, after the race festivities were over, Julie flew back through Cincinnati, Ohio, to visit Aunt Dorothy, her daughter Ann Hawley Patty and her family, and then on to Minnesota to visit her mother's mother. She didn't win the air race, but she gained an entirely new set of experiences.

A Chance to Pilot a Twin

Attesting to the concentration with which she pursued her ratings, Julie passed her flight tests for Certificated Flight Instructor on 14 October 1976. Within two weeks, she was challenged to become multi-engine rated.

While Julie was flying the T-34 in the Visalia, California area, she was approached by a man who was looking for a pilot to fly prisoners for the local Visalia Prison. He proposed the transport of prisoners to and from Visalia in a twin-engine Rockwell Aero Commander.

"In order to pilot a twin, I would have to get a multi-engine (ME) rating. I asked, 'Would you hire me if I were to get the rating?'

"He told me I would have to get the training in an Aero Commander, then he stipulated, "…an Aero Commander 500."

"I agreed, 'Okay, would you hire me if I get the training?' and he said he'd certainly consider it."

Julie knew full well the cost of getting the rating. It didn't require a great number of flying hours – a minimum of ten. But each flight hour in a multi-engine aircraft cost at least one hundred dollars. It was even more expensive to train in the Aero Commander 500 than in a Piper Apache or a Comanche.

Once again "Jule's Clocks" came to her rescue, helping to finance her investment in herself. She said, "I would tell those in charge at NAS Lemoore that I was taking a T-34 to pick up some parts. I would file a flight plan – what they termed an 'event' – and I would take the back seat out of the Beech to make room for some clocks. It cost money to make money, so this was my way to be enterprising. I really wanted bigger and better flying jobs."

A Commander 500 was available for training in San Carlos, so Julie commuted in a Navy T-34 between Lemoore and San Carlos Airport. R.J. Jones, the flight instructor who had given her the instrument rating earlier, trained her in multi-engine flight.

"R.J. really let out a yell," she said, "if you weren't precisely on speed and on the numbers (holding the designated altitude and heading to within 5 degrees and maintaining the assigned speed to within 5 knots). He'd yell, 'Take it around! Take it around!' You had to be just perfect! San Carlos' runway was only 2,600 feet in length and it was important to be exacting and under complete control. My multi-engine rating was added to my Commercial Certificate on 31 October 1976.

"The ink wasn't even dry on the certificate when I carried it by hand to Visalia. I showed the guy my logbooks, told him of the training I'd taken, and told him I'd sincerely like the job.

"It only took the man one second to look me up and down and to dismiss me with, 'I can't hire you.'

"I wanted to scream. 'What do you mean? Why in the world *not?*'

"He answered, 'You're too little. I can't hire some woman your size. What if a prisoner got loose, and tried to overpower you and take over the airplane? I can't risk hiring anybody like you.'"

This was not the last of Julie's discouraging interviews for flying jobs, but it was a crushing blow to one who had put out the money in good faith. One more time a man decided a woman couldn't hack it. Angry and upset, she hated having to admit to Rick that her multi-engine training had come to nothing. She didn't know whether to cry or to rage in fury. *Don't they think women can do anything?*

Not long after, one cooler day for Lemoore, when a steady breeze pushed the fingers of fog over the flight line, flying ground to a standstill. Julie answered the

85

telephone at Base Operations to an urgent male voice inquiring, "I'm calling from Agri-Till, here in Five Points, California. Do you have a pilot who could talk to me? I need to have agricultural machinery parts delivered for me."

Julie answered, "Well, I'm the only one here today, but I'm a pilot. What do you need?"

"How much flight time do you have?"

"Not much," Julie admitted. "Want me to fly to Five Points to meet you?"

She took a Navy T-34, did some scud running and miraculously found her way to what amounted to nothing more than a dirt strip at the confluence of five streets. For a few hairy moments in and out of the obscuring fog, she thought, "What in hell am I doing out here?"

Then she found the airstrip and put the T-34 down smoothly.

The man asked, "Does the Navy know you have that airplane out here?"

"No," Julie again admitted. "But, I want the job you're offering." She explained about getting her multi-engine rating for a guy in Visalia who led her to believe she would be hired and then turned her down flat. "What kind of flying do you want me to do?"

Agri-Till is a worldwide company; it boasts a large fleet of tractors suitable for agriculture, construction, and forestry uses and makes available a wide variety of makes and models of agricultural equipment to customers in California, Arizona, and the western states. The representative told her, "You'd be flying farm equipment between farmers and a repair facility. At the moment we're delivering parts for tomato harvesters and I need a pilot to fly the parts from various farm locations to be repaired and then returned to the owners. Your job would be to fly to designated farms, pick up damaged parts and collect the money, and then to fly the parts to the repair facility. Later, the repaired parts have to be returned. I have two Cessna 310s with a single seat in each of them leaving lots of room for spare parts. You can have that seat if you want the job."

Julie flew for Agri-Till for a year. She said, "I accumulated a lot of multi-engine time, and I never landed on any runways. I often wondered, 'Shall I go over those power lines or under them?' It was dangerous flying. I might be told, 'Fly to the Avenal VOR (very high frequency omni range, a navigational aid), fly eight miles to the south, there will be a green pickup truck parked next to the road. Land into the wind on the road by the pickup. Sometimes you'd land right on the side of an upgraded hill, knowing the upslope would help you to come to a stop."

On a hazard level equal to the low, obstacle-avoidance flying known to agricultural spray plane pilots, Julie's year of off-airport landings made her even more careful and precise. She couldn't have managed putting a multi-engine aircraft down on simply any ditch bank, dirt road, farm track, or field without having maintained precise speed and directional controls. More than once she was grateful for R.J. Jones' demands for accuracy.

"The 310, gutted out and capable of carrying the big hydraulic rams used in harvesters, which inevitably seemed to be the broken parts, was perpetually over gross weight," she explained. "A couple of times I had to land on the ditch bank adjacent to an aqueduct. Rick thought the flying was dangerous and he urged me to quit. Eventually, I decided it was only a matter of time before my luck would run out. I set a goal and decided I would quit after about 300 flying hours and do something else. I didn't have another job lined up, but I finally told my boss I was through. I'd had enough."

Although some speak of the "school of hard knocks," Julie profited from the demanding and dangerous flying. She learned her way around her native California as few ever have and it is to her credit she kept at it for so long.

Transporting Tiny Babies

Always watching for opportunities, she heard of a chance to fly incubator babies for Valley Children's Hospital in a Cessna 421 out of Western Sierra, a Fixed Base Operation on the Fresno airport. Julie applied and was pulled into another demanding job – a tense rescue mission. It consisted of transporting endangered babies to hospitals capable of handling their particular survival problems and kept a pilot on call all hours of the day and night.

"I thought I'd died and gone to heaven with this job – it paid well, the air-planes were big Cessna 421 or 414 twins, and the takeoffs and landings were always from paved runways. That in itself was a novelty after flying for Agri-Till.

"Being on call, I quickly found I was a slave to my beeper. I never knew what it was like to go out and have fun, which wasn't easy on our marriage. So many times Rick would say, 'Hey, we're going to a squadron party tonight,' and I'd have to say, 'I *can't*. I'm on call.' I didn't want to go to a party and be tempted to have a drink or two. Incubator babies are born around the clock and, if the beeper went off, so did I! It was like being a fighter pilot on alert and having to 'scramble' a jet at the sound of the siren. At the sound of the beeper, I'd rush to the airport and, if it was after normal hours, I'd jump on the tug, pull out either the Cessna 414 or the Cessna 421 and dash through a quick pre-flight check. I'd been accustomed to wrestling small training planes, but the C-414 weighed just over 4,000 pounds empty and the C-421 weighed over 4,200 pounds in the same configuration. It took a bit of work to inch them out of the hangar safely. But, what pretty flying machines! They had terrific power, responsive controls, and I loved to hear the throaty growl of the engine when I fired up and to see the ground drop away quickly when I took off."

Tension mounted. "When I was on call, my time was never my own. If I went to a coffee shop and ordered a cheese sandwich, inevitably the beeper would sound, whirling red lights would spin in the distance, an ambulance siren would squeal, and I'd have to say, 'Here's your money. Keep the sandwich. I've got to *go!*'

"I'd get the right engine running, the door open, and be ready to take off in minutes. Rain, fog, cold aside, what mattered were the lives of those babies."

Julie was compassionate and she found it impossible to maintain an objectivity toward the babies entrusted to her. The airplane, which was configured for the emergency with a litter and with incubator connections, generally carried the little patient along with a life support physician and another medical expert.

"They'd strap in the incubator and away we'd go."

But it wasn't always so straightforward. "I was reprimanded at one point about 'getting too involved with the babies,'" she said. "I would help to load them, would ask what was wrong with them, whether they were boys or girls, and what kind of chances the helpless little things might have. We picked up a newborn girl in Bakersfield one day and were trying to rush her back to Fresno. The weather had closed in, fog shrouding Fresno like a thick woolly blanket, dropping the instrument minima to zero-zero. Part 135 Federal Aviation Regulations (FARs) called for an additional pilot if weather conditions required actual instrument flying for more than fifteen minutes. But, in the high pressure flight arena, it was more than likely I was solo and this was one of those times. Despite the below minima report, I attempted an instrument landing. I descended and reached the minimum altitude before even entering the thick fog obscuring the airport.

"I said aloud, 'This isn't going to work.' It was awful. I was completely frustrated as I knew we needed to get onto the ground for the baby. I turned to the medic on board and said, 'I know from my experience at Navy Lemoore that I can land there. I could do a GCA approach, which is ground controlled by radar through actual radar observers. I've done it before. They could do that for us.

"The medic refused, saying that it was strictly against regulations to land at a military base. 'That's not authorized,' he said.

"We could save this baby's life if we gave it a try," Julie protested.

She shot a couple of approaches into Fresno and then gave in to the inevitable. "I can't get into Visalia; I can't get into Fresno. We'll have to go back to Bakersfield."

"Never mind," the doctor said. "The baby just expired."

Julie felt sick. To heap insult upon injury, her boss questioned her wisdom in trying to land at the military base when she saw him the next morning. "What is this about trying to put the twin down at Navy Lemoore?" he demanded.

"I told him I was completely familiar with the base, its approaches, and that I even knew the controllers who would be giving us the ground-controlled approach. 'I think we might have had a chance to save the little girl.'"

He said, "Your job is to climb aboard the airplane when the ambulance is on its way, get those engines started, and fly. You don't even need to know the sex of the baby. You got that?'"

Unfriendly Skies

Visibilities, ceilings, and demanding bosses were only part of Julie's worries. Rick came home in a foul mood one evening, admitting the Navy had included his name in a RIF – a military Reduction in Force known in modern parlance as "downsizing." He would be cut from the Navy within a week. The pain was softened somewhat with a separation allowance, but the reality was an immediate loss of position and salary. Marriages have to survive, as stated in the vows, the better and the worse. But, 'the worse' can sometimes cause damage that is insidious and slow to surface.

Rick and his fellow naval aviators made arrangements to obtain equivalent Federal Aviation Administration civilian licenses and ratings for those they held in the military. Unfamiliar with the civilian rules and requirements, Julie coached him and several of his buddies to help them pass the written exams. Having worked as hard and having spent as much money and time as she had to obtain her certificates, Julie couldn't help but feel resentful of Rick's Navy training and simply having to accept civilian equivalency in certification to be eligible to fly with U.S. airlines. Not long after having left the Navy, Rick received offers from more than one airline. He opted to go with Hughes Air West. Hired as a Flight Engineer (FE), Rick was notified he would be based in Las Vegas, Nevada.

"He was getting the airline career and I was the one with the airline ties. I knew it was because his military training was exemplary, but I couldn't help but smart over a career path denied to me as a woman. A few women had been hired, but the airlines were very reluctant to even *talk* to women pilots. I was happy for Rick, but I resented his chance to fly with the airline my father had flown when its doors were closed to me."

CHAPTER EIGHT: *ALASKAN WINGS*

Despite the threat of having to deal with one lecherous boss who flamboyantly cruised the California streets in his flashy, red convertible, Julie had accepted the offer of becoming a flight instructor at the Fresno-based Fixed Base Operation, Western Sierra, while she and Rick were living in Lemoore. She was forewarned of the boss' wandering eye. However, the method of her hiring was intriguing and the compelling reality of earning money and accruing flight experience were impossible to refuse.

"I flew the Rockwell Commander I'd leased back to the Naval Aero Club into Fresno one gray day. When I got home my telephone was ringing off the hook. The man on the phone was offering me a job, explaining having heard me on the aircraft radio during my communications with Fresno Tower. I had been taking an instrument (IFR) clearance prior to departure and, in a method mysterious to me, he must have checked up on me with the tower controllers or through the registration of my aircraft. However it was done, he ferreted out my name, address, and telephone number.

"When he called, he said, 'We're hiring some instructor and charter pilots and you sound very professional. If you hold a CFI, we'd like to hire you as a flight instructor here at Fresno Air Terminal.' This was in the winter of 1976. I flew up to Fresno and was hired on the spot.

"Others warned me about the guy, but I was young and I was married; I assumed a wedding band would mean 'hands off.' I had a lesson to learn."

Julie started as a flight instructor, but her boss requested her upgrade into his charter department, most flights of which were accomplished with solo pilots. In the case of inclement weather, Western Sierra's policy required two pilots aboard.

Julie hadn't flown charter very long before two of the Fresno aircraft were sent to the same destination and, as the weather was IFR, four pilots were dispatched. The boss climbed aboard with Julie. A menacing gray-black cloud cover thickened and darkened during the flight, solidifying into an impenetrable mass of clouds. A return flight was impossible. All four pilots stranded in Bakersfield had to "RON" – Remain Over Night.

"We found a hotel," she explained, "and it was almost as if this guy planned on lousy weather getting us grounded away from home. He came onto me, got pushy and demanding, and wanted me to let him into my hotel room. This treatment was new to me. He was outside my door, pounding on it and I hunkered down between the two beds in the hotel room and dialed Rick. I whispered, 'He's after me. He's at my door right now.'

"'Whatever you do,' Rick told me, 'don't let him in!'

"The stand-off worked and, when he left in disgust, I finally was able to climb into bed and get some rest. The next morning, the four of us flew back to Fresno. He was as cold as ice and barely a word was spoken in our cockpit. However, after we'd landed, he told me to report to his office. There he announced, 'We don't need you in this charter department any more. You're finished.'"

She was floored. It took a moment to digest his words. *Finished. I'm fired?*

When she asked, 'Can't I be placed back in the Flight Instruction Department under Jack Nyce?' He was adamant. 'No. We have no need of you any more.'

"I fully understood the reason and it made me angry. I felt powerless. It was hard enough to be unemployed, but I knew that being fired wouldn't look good on my résumé. *How could I combat it? If I did take legal steps to get the job back, couldn't he make life miserable for me?*"

Flight Engineer

"Rick made a good suggestion. He said, 'You've wanted the time to get your Flight Engineer written tests out of the way. Maybe this is your chance.'"

Julie attended Bill Phelp's Accelerated Ground School in Burlingame for a two-week course during February 1977. At the completion of the ground school preparation, she took the FAA written exams. Focusing on turboprop, turbojet, and reciprocating aircraft, she passed two written tests – the only requirements to obtaining the ratings – and added Flight Engineer Basic and Flight Engineer Turbo to her growing array of certificates.

She also called Jack Nyce, the manager of the Flight Instruction Department at Western Sierra. To her relief, Nyce lived up to the homonym of his name and was glad to welcome Julie back to her original job as a flight instructor within his department. *What a relief.* She knew of the political upheaval of the 1960s leading to the major changes of the 1970s. She knew about the civil rights movement, the feminist movement, and the opportunities for claiming sexual harassment. They would have given her a chance to legally demand a return to her position. But, as a competent and experienced pilot and an excellent flight instructor, she proved her capabilities instead of casting about for legal ways to force her way in. She focused on her value to the company and grabbed Jack Nyce's offer immediately.

While Rick eyed his airline career, Julie stayed with Western Sierra, zealously adding many flight hours to her logbooks and expanding her experience to make herself better prepared as an airline pilot. She knew where she wanted to go. She just wasn't sure whether she would be allowed to get there. She wondered if women would *ever* be accepted fully and widely as competent professional pilots.

Happy Herb Flights

Some of her experience came in the form of charter flights for Western Sierra, gambling junkets between Fresno and Reno, Nevada, its logo beaming an unmistakably happy grin from a wide, round face. Originally invented by a graphic artist in Worcester, Massachusetts, the cheery smile put its viewers into happy

93

frames of mind. Happy Herb's logo was a smiley face before it became legion throughout the United States.

But Julie recalled how the gamblers shied away from climbing aboard an aircraft piloted by a woman. "When customers came out to the airplanes wearing a smiley face on their jackets, you knew they had paid for a Happy Herb flight. Sometimes it would be a day flight and we'd fly to Reno and return. Sometimes we'd have to stay overnight and I'd have to share a room with the male pilots, a policy adopted to minimize expense to the company.

"When I first started flying the Happy Herb flights, none of the clients wanted to fly with me. My airplane was always the last to fill up. Most of the passengers were regulars and they began to get to know me. Pretty soon, they would fight to get into my airplane. I'd let them drink booze and sometimes I'd roll the airplane on the way to Reno, just for the fun of it. Sometimes Rick would fly with us, if he was available and if there was an empty seat. In that case, we'd get our own hotel room.

"Herb did not own his airplanes. He chartered them from Western Sierra. Some of the other pilots would tease, if they saw me roll with my passengers aboard. 'We're going to tell Herb on you.' I shrugged it off and they'd follow up with, 'Can you teach me how to do a roll?' Those flights were crazy and they were fun. A charter pilot wore a lot of hats – pilot, baggage handler, weather briefer, and gofer. My only complaint was feeling a lot of pressure to go ahead with the flights even if something came up with the airplane – alternator failure or something. I hated to be pressured to take a flight when I knew there was a reason the airplane should be grounded."

The Girl From San Joaquin

The charter piloting with Western Sierra proved to be the springboard to new opportunities for Julie. During one overnight in Bakersfield, she had gotten into a conversation with a fellow who told her he was headed for an interview with Golden West Airlines.

"They fly Canadian de Havilland Twin Otters," he said. "It's a good place to get a start. What can you lose? They're hiring. They're a good company. Why not apply?"

"I'd heard of Golden West; I knew they had a commuter operation in San Francisco," she admitted. "So, I called the managerial offices of Golden West for an interview.

"When I was told, 'You know, we've never hired a woman.' I was quiet for a minute." *Was I supposed to figure the policy was carved in stone and irrefutable? Was I just supposed to hang up and let it go?*

A week or so later, she called the offices again. This time she was told, "We would entertain your application, but there is a prerequisite. Before you can even arrange an interview with us, you'll have to attend ground school from the product support team of de Havilland in Toronto, Canada."

Toronto, Canada? How could she afford to travel so far, invest so much, and take time from flying to attend a course in *Canada?* There were no guarantees she'd be hired even if she successfully completed the course! She thought, "Oh, God. Forget it! I don't have the money."

Anger can be a great motivator, if a person directs any rage toward worthwhile goals. Julie approached her bank officials to apply for a loan. "If I didn't believe in myself, how could I expect others to believe in me?"

Granted the loan, Julie flew to Canada and settled in to one of the hardest classes she had ever taken. Designed to instruct crewmembers in the operation of the de Havilland DHC-6, the ten-year-old aircraft first introduced on 20 May 1965, the course was specifically geared to those who fly the Twin Otter in the Canadian bush. It went far beyond the relatively straightforward systems and operation of the aircraft. As in her pursuit of the multi-engine rating, she might be disappointed by a rejection by the management at Golden West when the course of study was complete; however, the ME rating was well worth its cost. At the very least, having taken ground training in Toronto would represent achievement.

"In Toronto, I was in a class filled with guys, some of them from the States, but also from Europe and, of course, Canada," she said. "Most were accustomed to handling their own needs in the remote areas of Canada: they flew their own airplanes, fueled their own airplanes, and maintained their own airplanes. They had to know the Twin Otter from its nose to its tail, inside and out. The course was tough. I got through it, but it was very, very difficult. It was a product support school held for those who needed and wanted to learn everything about the aircraft there was to know.

"There were questions like, 'How many microns of thickness are required for the oil cooler exchange unit?' Particles are sized in microns. A hair from your head is about 60 to 75 microns in diameter and, when the particles are less than 35 microns, they are not visible to the naked eye. This kind of information is essential to the mechanic or the expert in filters who is responsible for protecting a system from contaminants, but it was purely rote memorization for me. I passed, but it was really challenging.

"And the graduation certificate was no guarantee. I held the piece of parchment, but I had no promises of being hired as an air crew member. Even with the course behind me, I was less than halfway there."

Her search to be hired by a United States airline led to filing applications with *thirty* companies! Julie's tactics changed as rejections accumulated. Having attached a photograph when it was indicated, Rick suggested dropping the photo from her applications. She stopped any admission of her femininity and skipped the square that called for sexual identification, signing some of her applications with the name *Julian*. Why advertise being a woman when it is an undeniable truth once you walk into the office for an interview?

"It wasn't so much being qualified," she said, "getting the first interview was the hardest part of getting hired. I was told it was easy for the airlines to toss an application from a woman into the wastebasket. I tried to be persistent and determined. I kept updating my flying time and notifying the various lines of any new certificates, ratings, or flight experience to prove my serious interested in being an airline pilot. I wanted my name to become familiar to those in charge of hiring.

"Out of the thirty airlines to which I submitted an application, I was invited for an interview to four: American, Continental, Western, and Hughes Airwest. My interview with American was a disaster. I was flown to the headquarters in Dallas; but, unwittingly, I failed to carry the requisite chocolate and flowers that the male applicants made a practice of offering to the Chief Pilot's secretary. I was the only female applicant in the room and I hadn't been clued in on what was expected. The secretary took one look at me, determined that I was too short and told me to wait. I sat for six hours in the outer office, never getting as much as a look at the chief pilot.

"With Golden West, it took nine *months* before I had a chance to be interviewed by the chief, Abe August. One time, when I put through a call to Golden West, I heard the fellow who answered the phone lean away from the receiver and say, 'It's the Girl from San Joaquin.' I didn't have a name, but at least I was becoming identifiable!"

Airline management couldn't hold out much longer. The handwriting was on the wall. Internationally, women started taking to airliners in the 1950s: in India – Prem Mathur was hired as a pilot as early as 1951; in Bulgaria, Maria Atansova was hired in 1953; and in Scandinavia, Turi Wideroe was hired in 1969. Even airlines in North America were being compelled to follow suit. In 1973: Emily Howell Warner was hired in January by Frontier Airlines, Rosella Bjornson was hired in April in Canada, and Bonnie Tiburzi was hired in May by American Airlines. It was time to give a chance to "the Girl from San Joaquin."

Ernie Clark's Airline

On the home front, Rick had already been hired to fly with Julie's dad's airline which now had become Hughes Airwest. Having pulled up the roots planted in Lemoore, Rick and Julie decided to buy a home on a lake in Morgan Hill, California, a small town twelve miles south of San Jose in the Santa Clara Valley. Surrounded by beautiful mountains, the quaint city maintained its small town flavor in its cupped valley formed by the Santa Cruz range to the west and the

Diablo Mountains on the east.

Based out of Las Vegas, Rick planned to commute between San Francisco and Vegas. The picturesque spot he and Julie chose had previously attracted Rick's mother and stepfather, Janet and George Noonan.

Julie and Rick were two assertive people trying to wrest the most out of their careers. They gave of themselves to the flying, to the training, the flight hours, and to the separations they found increasingly demanding. As more of their interest and energy was directed toward aviation, their marriage began to suffer.

"We got together whenever I could fly to see him or he could fly to see me," Julie said. "It was a tough deal. I wanted to get my career going, too. We spent two years in Lemoore and those were happy years."

Golden West

Perhaps both of the Ames could be happy again. Julie was at last notified by the Chief Pilot, Captain Abel August, that she and other applicants – all male – were to be flight tested in a Twin Otter. On 24 June 1977, Julie was going to get her big chance! It wasn't as if small single-engine and twin-engine aircraft would be brushed aside as things of her past. Not at all. Julie had fallen in love with flying. She loved being airborne, being in control of her own destiny and the destiny of her passengers. She longed for a role in the airlines. Longed for her own place in the sky.

Here was her opportunity to fly! At the time of the check flights, the male applicants were all sent to fly en masse with Swing Lindsey, a check pilot.

"They singled me out to fly alone with Abe. Cool Swing Lindsey, with his stogie and his laid back manner, was going to load the guys into a DHC 6," Julie said, "and they were going to fly out to Catalina Island, do some holding patterns, some instrument procedures and , in general, have a 'good, old boys' check-out. My check ride was different. In the first place, I would be alone with Abe, the check pilot. In addition, Abe stuttered badly in every situation except when he was using an airplane radio. Transmitting clearly, his voice showed no trace of stutter like country singer and song composer great, Mel Tillis, who sang with no speech impediment at all. Yet, it was difficult to go through the ground portion of the flight and to struggle to avoid filling in words or otherwise offending a truly great pilot and fine man.

"I had to fly under the hood to simulate instrument conditions with Abe. The first thing we did was a holding pattern over the Catalina VOR. If I'd been with all the other guys and hadn't been first up to the plate, I could have watched the way the others flew. It would have settled my ideas and helped to get my nerves under control. As it was, I started to turn the wrong way. Abe told me, 'Think about what you are doing.'

"'I *am*,' I told him. Then I realized I was turning left instead of making the required right turns expected of holding patterns. I said, 'Sir, I made a mistake. Can I fly back to the fix and start over again?'

"'No problem,' Abe said, easily.

"I knew I could do better, but I was extremely nervous. Making a mistake didn't help at all. Although every fiber of my being was trying to do the very best job I could, I couldn't help but compare my check out with the ones that I imagined was being given to the guys. I figured that they were taking their turns, getting a chance to watch each other at the controls, see what it was the check pilot was going to require, and how he handled the aircraft, too. I imagined they were having a high old time while I was on my own. I was so keyed up I was making mistakes. I felt angry with myself. I *knew* better!

"To make the pain even greater, once we had landed and the stress of the check ride was over, the male pilots were all hired. They were taken aboard, sent to be fitted for their uniforms, given their physical exams, and set up with training dates. Captain August told me, 'I have a problem with your hair.'"

Captain Abel August was admired by all who had flown with him. He was undoubtedly fair. The trouble was he'd never hired a *woman*. It must have been difficult for him to hire the first.

"My *hair*," she repeated. "My *hair?*"

Julie was born a brunette; hers was silken, fine brown waist-length hair, generally worn tied back. She frowned and asked, "What would you like me to *do* with my hair?"

Told, "It has to go. When you've cut it, come back and we'll talk some more."

Julie shortened her hairstyle into a page boy, despite some criticism at home. She and Rick had a bit of a go-around over something one found trivial and the other deemed important. It was a classic small problem that mushroomed into something larger. Or, like a metal fatigue crack in a wing that shows up only in a diagnostic eddy current testing, perhaps small fissures lurked below the surface compromising the strength of their marriage.

Alaska Beckons

In a more assertive demonstration of her growing independence, Julie was intrigued by an ad for the sale of surplus airplanes. "I was sitting at home, waiting for a flight. I had a beeper on and was reading *Trade-a-Plane*. An ad jumped out at me. 'For Sale: Auction by U.S. Government, two Civil Air Patrol (CAP) A-45s located in Anchorage, Alaska.' I thought, 'Wow. Who would read that and know it means two Beech T-34 Mentors? The average pilot doesn't know that military designation.'

"The minimum bid was $17,000. All I could think was how much I'd enjoyed flying the T-34 at NAS Lemoore and how sad I'd felt to pull the mixture back to cut the engine after my last flight. I sat in the quiet cockpit for a few minutes and thought, 'I'll never have another chance to fly one of these airplanes again.'

"Penny Becker , a pilot, a member of The Ninety-Nines, and a friend to whom I'd given a familiarization ride at Western Sierra, was the first person I called. Penny was my air race co-pilot when we got together to compete and bring home some trophies. Penny was 'Captain Ground' and I was 'Captain Air.' We always chose race number 11 because it was easy to paste onto the tail of whatever plane we flew and it was Penny's lucky number. Later, Penny was with me when I flew to the Salton Sea to take my seaplane rating in 1978. We both marveled when I trained and tested for floatplane flying and never even climbed high enough to see *zero* on the altimeter. Like Death Valley, the Salton Sea is below sea level; actually, it is 139 feet below sea level. Training and testing in a Piper Cub on floats, none of my water takeoffs and landings took me high enough to get out of the negative numbers.

"I called Penny and told her how much I'd like to bid on the surplus airplanes in Alaska. When I lamented not having $17,000, she told me I didn't need to pay that amount to register the bid. Then she went one better. She found the necessary $1,000 to place the bid and she loaned me the money."

Without breathing a word of her plans to Rick, Julie placed the bid and promptly forgot about it. Wasn't it unwise to bring up the possibility of buying a T-34 before there was any certainty that, when the auction was over, she might be the highest bidder? It was a challenge to judge the timing for broaching a sensitive subject with a spouse when even a haircut and spending time together proved to be controversial. *Why not wait to talk about it when it looked as if the bid might actually win? Why start some sort of battle when the bid might come to nothing?*

At the time, Rick's hiring by Hughes Airwest and what she perceived to be his fabulous flying assignments intensified her desire to be hired. She focused on getting on with an airline, not fully appreciating that her hiring would speed up the graveyard spiral of her already strained marriage.

More Hair Has to Go

Having kept herself busy during the intervening weeks between her interviews with Abe August, Julie was surprised to hear her hair was still too long. Abe told her, "I *still* have a problem with the hair. If you want to be a flight officer for Golden West Airlines, the hair has to be as short as mine." He gestured with his hand, bringing it alongside his ear. "It has to be *short!*"

He continued, "Also, there's another major problem. No women have been in and out of our Operations area. It's on the ramp and located between runways at Los Angeles International – LAX. It has a men's room conveniently placed for

pilots who are arriving and departing and need a quick stop in the head. But, the restroom lacks a door. How are we going to handle it when you come barreling into Ops to pick up papers, get weather, meet your captain, and some guy's using the toilet?"

Julie was quick. She never batted an eye as she said, "I'll cut my hair short

1977 was a good year, Julie is hired by Golden West

and I'll buy a damn door. I'll even pay for the door's installation, if you'll give me this job." She put her hand over her mouth and said, "I'm sorry. That just slipped out."

He smiled and said, "I like your spunk. When can you start?"

At Last

Julie never forgot Captain Abel August giving her the first big break! She became the first and only woman pilot hired to fly with Golden West Airlines, smoothly transitioning into the First Officer position without a lot of unnecessary publicity or media hoopla. She noted, much later, "I never did have to buy that john door."

Having resigned at Western Sierra, last flying with them on 23 June 1977, she flew preparatory training flights with Golden West's Don Singleton on the first, second, and on the fourth of July. She flew a check ride with Swing Lindsey, noting in her logbook, "Great Captain," and took off for 4.7 flight hours on 8 July 1977, her first day of a momentous year.

On 12 July 1977, she joined another "great captain," Bob Naylor, and logged two landings and two approaches. Now she had to prove she was as adept at flying as any of the other new hires. Or better.

She rather enjoyed being the only woman among 110 male pilots. The open bathroom became a joke. At first, she'd knock three times and say, "Julie," warning of her entrance to anyone who might be indisposed. In the typical camaraderie of airline ops offices, guys started mimicking her – knocking three times and saying, in a sing-song falsetto, "Ju-lee." It got to be a joke.

The first woman pilot with Golden West and, ultimately, the only.

The flying, on the other hand, was rugged. "Flying around California in a Twin Otter at 130 knots in bad weather and hopping through leg after leg all day," she said. "Well, that got old in no time. I'd come home dead on my feet.

"I was based in Los Angeles (LAX) because I was on reserve. Sometimes I'd have to cover Ventura, drive to Santa Barbara, leaving at 2 a.m. to catch the first flight at 5; or I could be down as far as Orange County Airport. The commute *to* and *from* the airport was wicked. However, I did love being the little queen bee to all of the Golden West pilots. They were wonderful to me; they looked after me and made the job special.

"My home-away-from-home was also another story. I lived in a ratty $425 per month apartment. I wasn't too crazy about it and Rick hated it. He didn't like visiting me in Los Angeles and we saw each other too infrequently. Our already strained marriage was pushed to the edge. While I flew out of LAX, he flew out of Vegas. We called Morgan Hill home, and sometimes we'd get together there. Sometimes I'd get to Vegas to see him, but even our days off worked against us. They often differed and the strain was obvious.

"Most of my flying was out and back, out and back – in and out of LAX to Ventura, Santa Monica, Ontario, Orange County, always returning to Los Angeles. I put in a request to fly the mail at night and was teamed with a guy named J.J. Quinn. I was warned that J.J. would complain of a bad back and would never help me load or unload the mail, but I wanted that job. It was steady, predictable, and paid better than regular passenger carrying."

At the outset, the first night mail flight together was grim. J.J. couldn't believe he'd been paired with a woman and he wasn't a bit happy about it. But Julie Clark isn't just *any* woman. She is a worker and, when a job has to be done, she goes at it with a vengeance. She'd load 1,600 pounds of mail, if it was required. She said, "I often did it without J.J.'s help; I loaded on one end and then unloaded the same mail at the destination – although there was generally someone at the other end who would help me.

"Our route of flight was to Palmdale, then up to China Lake where we spent the night in a bunk house provided by Operations. Our first night there, I looked at the bunk beds thinking, 'Oh, my God' as I put on a nightgown and kept my airline jacket over it.

"J.J. asked, in a crusty voice, 'Do you want the top bunk or the bottom?'

"I told him, 'I'll just take the top, sir.' Then, as I climbed up, I thought, 'Why did I say the top? He can look up my nightgown while I'm getting up here!'

"As if he was reading my mind, J.J. said, 'Don't worry. I'm not looking.'

"We got used to the arrangement and, eventually, J.J. ended up being one of my good friends. From China Lake in the morning, we'd depart. J.J. would go to his home and I would fly passengers until my time limit at noon. Then I'd have a few hours off and have a repeat night mail flight in the evening with J.J. again. I burned candles at both ends and logged a lot of multiengine turboprop time; precious hours filled my logbook and added to all I was learning."

Networking, a vast spider web of interconnected strings of data, is a lifeline within the aviation industry. Opportunities Julie capitalized upon were complex chances brought to her attention by her husband, her co-workers, her flying buddies, and her friends. John Mayhew, whom she'd known when he was employed at Martin Aviation, a Fixed Base Operation in Orange County, was the friend who told her of an opportunity to get a rating in the Cessna Citation business jet. He told her about having been hired by National Jet Industries, saying, "after obtaining my Citation Type Rating, I was hired as a jet flight instructor."

Never one to let a possibility pass, Julie visited National Jet Industries, which agreed to provide her with jet training in exchange for her agreement to stay on with them for a year as an instructor. On 23 and 24 September 1977, Julie added the C-500 Citation Type Rating to her certificates. In so doing, she was committing for a year as an instructor.

She actually only instructed ground school and flew a couple of charter flights, working for National Jet Industries on the sly while flying for Golden West. She knew Abe and Swing would eventually find out. Aviation is a relatively small field. The same interconnectedness bringing vital and desirable news along invisible wires also broadcasts information we'd just as soon remained secret.

An Alaskan Bird

Another secret seeking the light of day was the response to the bid Julie made for the T-34, the "Warbird in Alaska." She was notified about holding the winning bid! It was imperative that she travel to Alaska to pay for and remove the aircraft.

"I'd almost forgotten about having made the bid," she said. "When word came that I was to come to Alaska to fly it away, I was stunned. But, the shock was much greater to Rick. He'd known nothing about the bidding process. When I was notified of having won, the first person that I called – again – was Penny Becker. She went from bank to credit union to bank with me, trying to find one single loan officer who was daring enough to risk a loan. When they asked, 'Where is the airplane?' I told them 'Alaska.' To, 'What is its condition?' I told them I hadn't seen it. They asked, 'What is its Blue Book value?' and I had to tell them, 'surplus military equipment *has* no Blue Book rating.' No wonder the loan officers refused! It was amazing we finally found one trusty soul at Crocker Bank in Fresno who was willing to take the risk. Loaned $14,000, I breathed a huge sigh of relief."

The next in line, who wanted both T-34s, was an aircraft restorer named Red Stevenson in Tulsa, Oklahoma. "As I was the highest bidder, I got to choose between the two. I called the maintenance people to ask their advice and was told one plane 'looked better,' but the other was more 'mechanically sound.' Knowing that Red Stevenson wanted 'my' airplane, too, the pressure was on for me to get to Alaska. I had to tell Rick where I was going and what I was doing.

"The roof went off the scale! It was *ugly*. I doubted he even cared whether I made it back or not."

She was flying for Golden West on 12 July 1977 and two days later, on 14 July, she arrived at Merrill Field in Anchorage via Western Airlines. Early the next morning, she awoke to cold, depressing rain and fog and hired a taxi for Elmendorf Air Force Base to locate "her" T-34A. The military logos had been scraped off; however, the craft was an aluminum relative of the planes she'd been flying at Navy Lemoore. There were subtle differences between the A and the B models and all she had flown were T-34Bs. Although she knew the T-34B well, she didn't know *this* T-34A at all.

Warned of a need for survival gear, a gun, and emergency rations of food and water, Penny again came to her rescue, renting the equipment at a sporting goods store and having it shipped to Anchorage. Julie added some charts and navigational aids to help her fly almost 3,000 miles in a yet unseen machine. Once in Alaska, the military told her she didn't need the equipment. They assured her she would be sitting on a complete survival kit located beneath her seat. She had to make arrangements to ship the equipment back to Penny.

Because the weather was below the minimums in which a pilot can legally fly according to Visual Flight Rules (VFR), her departure was held up for eight hours. When she finally departed, she flew through "Windy Pass" toward Whitehorse, Yukon. She got lost and finally determined, after aligning herself with the direction of a known runway, her wet compass was at least forty-five degrees off. In Whitehorse, she was grounded in very bad weather, low ceilings, and poor visibility. She spent a restless and uncomfortable night sleeping on the floor of the women's bathroom in the terminal building. Discovering that the compass in the rear seat was accurate, she borrowed some tools and used the correct compass to replace her front-seat gauge.

The next morning, Julie and the airplane left for Watson Lake, Yukon. During her careful preflight, she looked at the nose of the airplane, which lacked a grill to cover its carburetor air filter intake. This gaping hole reminded her of the lopsided smile of a friend named Wally from her TWA days. He had helped her to use an E6B computer at a time when few flight attendants were

A Civil Air Patrol surplus airplane comes home with Julie

taking flight lessons. Believing that every airplane should have a name, her T-34 immediately was christened. That afternoon, despite a rough engine, the duo limped on to McKenzie, British Columbia.

There, in a catastrophe, the battery blew! Julie explained, "A hole was blown through the side of the airplane. Battery acid leaked into the cockpit and, as the fumes spread, I was forced to land. The fumes were bad enough, but the acid splattered on my clothes. It ate portions of the zippers on my knee-high boots.

"Mechanics told me, 'The battery blew because of an overheat problem. We can get you started, but you're not going to have any electrical power.' How was the gear operated? Electrically. How were the flaps operated? Electrically. What did the radio depend upon? Electricity! I had to operate to Prince George, British Columbia, without a radio (NORDO).

"The rest of the flight was tough. Gear can be muscled down manually; but, even more challenging was that the gear couldn't be retracted. The extended gear created enormous drag all the way to California. Drag, in turn, forced the cylinder head temperatures almost to redline. The hotter the engine, the hotter the oil temps and the lower the oil pressure. All were indications that a pilot does *not* want to see. Flaps can be ignored, if precise airspeed control is maintained, so that was relatively minor. I had to navigate with nothing but a wet compass and a chart. But having no radio meant that I had to make telephone calls to tower operators ahead of my arrival to be expected in their airspace. I couldn't depend on the fact that there wouldn't be more surprises. I also had to count on landing at airports with the capability of giving me 24-volt power starts. That was a rarity. Most airports served aircraft that ran on 12-volt batteries.

"Personally, I looked awful. My clothes – the same ones in which I'd left home – were splattered and stained by the battery acid and my boots drooped toward my ankles like sloppy stockings. The airplane was a sight and my looks probably convinced people that we'd narrowly escaped a fate worse than death."

At Penticton, she savored a dinner and a rented room with a bed, luxuriating in this beautiful resort town. The luxury was short-lived. South of there, the flight was interrupted with a low oil pressure indication. She landed at Omak and there, she added five quarts of oil before pressing on to Kingsley Field, Klamath Falls, Oregon – a joint-use military and civilian base. At Kingsley, she landed first, and then had to explain to tower operators about her radio silence.

Despite oil problems, she pressed on to Red Bluff, California and, on 16 July, she reached Oroville, California. She had to clear customs on a very small dirt strip and flew on to Fremont and San Carlos. She landed at Fremont to call on a land line to obtain permission to land in San Carlos.

In her logbook, she wrote, "Home. Praise the Lord."

Airborne the Next Day

Amazingly and indicative of her prodigious energy level, Julie flew with Golden West the following two days with Captain Ron Reed. On 17 July 1977 she flew two hops and on 18 July, she flew four hops for a total of 5.3 hours of flying time.

The T-34A Mentor, "BEFORE!"

Her enthusiasm was boundless and, temporarily, confrontations at home were held at bay.

"When the battery acid fumes filled the cockpit, I thought, 'I'm dead!' Then, I sort of shrugged and figured, 'Oh, well. Rick's going to kill me anyway. He's going to have my ass on a platter.'

"I dreaded showing the airplane to him. It wasn't terrific mechanically, but it looked much worse than it was. I stopped in Fresno to see him, but I dreaded hearing his comments.

"He said, 'I can't believe you bought that. I can't believe you went all the way to Alaska and brought *this* back.'

"I was headed for Los Angeles; he was going back to Las Vegas. I got "Wally" home, but I didn't know where I was going to park it. I didn't have a tie-down site. I had to get back to Golden West; I had a furious husband. I knew he'd be right if he suggested, 'You brought this all on yourself.' It was another of the low points of my life."

Julie and her T-34 "Wally" had safely flown for 21 hours. But home wasn't ever going to be the same again. Did Rick, born on 1 November under the sign of Scorpio, fulfill the zodiac descriptions? "Scorpios are the most intense, profound, powerful characters in the zodiac. Even when they appear self-controlled and calm, there is a seething intensity of emotional energy under the placid exterior. They are like the volcano not far under the surface of a calm sea."

Rick was not perfect. Few persons are. But, Julie and her T-34 were pushing her Scorpio to his limits.

CHAPTER NINE: *A LEGACY REVISITED*

Julie's airline start was timely, a successful period for commuter lines like Golden West Airlines. In part, this was in thanks to the design of the Canadian de Havilland DH-6, the Twin Otter.

"The Third Level airline industry," according to U.S. Airlines' expert R.E.G. Davies in his *Airlines of the United States since 1914,* "found its first opportunities for expansion on a wide scale when such aircraft as the Twin Otter ...began to present a reasonably modern image to the public. ...During 1967 and 1968, the rapid expansion mushroomed and, by December 1968 a passenger could travel from Seattle to Miami entirely by Third Level carriers... [whose] routes became an elaborate affair, with concentration at the major hubs of New York, Chicago, Los Angeles, Dallas, Boston, and Seattle. ...The new airline breed boasted new equipment and did not ask for a penny of subsidy. The new aircraft were, of course, far more efficient than their predecessors. Had the early Local Service airlines possessed aircraft like the Twin Otter, airline history in the United States might have taken a different course.

"...By March 1969, a series of negotiations between several Third Level airlines in Southern California resulted in an important merger, the full significance of which is best illustrated by ...the rapid-fire ancestry of Golden West Airlines."

Davies went on to demonstrate graphically the small lines – Avalon, Catalina,

111

Aero Commuter, Skymark, and Cable Commuter – that merged to become Golden West Airlines. Golden West provided service for the state of California from the mountains westward and from Santa Rosa in the north to San Diego in

the south. It was in 1969 that the Third Level Airlines transitioned to be known as Commuter Air Carriers.

U.S. airliner history is rife with the mergers and acquisitions of smaller airlines by the larger. Periodic feeding frenzies – in quest of specific routes, particular equipment, and occasionally all of one line's assets – caused the small to be gobbled by the larger like open-mouthed sharks tore into schools of vulnerable fish.

As Golden West began with five smaller lines, Air West was formed in April 1968 with

Like father, like daughter, taking to an airplane Ernie flew

the merger of Pacific, Bonanza, and West Coast lines. Its debut was hailed with the slogan, "Now the West is One."

In the 1940s, Ernie Clark had participated in the formation of the line that became Pacific Air Lines in the mid-1950s. It was overwhelming for Julie to receive a notice inviting her to interview with the line that incorporated Pacific – Air West. The reclusive Howard Hughes purchased the airline in 1972 and changed the name to Hughes Airwest.

Julie was thrilled. To think of flying with her father's line, to fly the airplanes that her father flew, and to fly with some of the crew members with whom her father had flown was an opportunity beyond measure. Hughes Airwest served from Calgary and Alberta in Canada, from Seattle and throughout California, to Great Falls, Montana; Salt Lake City, Utah; Phoenix and Tucson, Arizona; and into Mexico. Its headquarters were established in San Francisco and its training and maintenance base was Phoenix.

Transition ensued. Julie had flown a total of 111 flight hours with Western

Sierra between 28 April and 23 June 1977. In the five months of employ with Golden West – from 24 June 1977 to 5 November 1977 – she logged 284 hours in the Twin Otter. As had so many airline pilot hopefuls, she used her experience at Golden West Airlines as a stepping stone to a bigger line. Having flown with the California commuter, she gained experience and demonstrated her capability as a line pilot. When she added her Citation type rating to her certificates, she furthered her talents, but there was a cost involved. While trying to live up to her commitment to National Jet Industries, she received her first invitations to be interviewed by larger airlines. Ironically, a telegram offered her a position with Western Airlines the same day she received her call from Hughes Airwest.

Yet, how could she refuse Hughes Airwest? Her husband had been hired nine months prior and this was unmistakably her big chance to fly with her father's airline and in the same airplanes in which her father flew! How enticing! Wouldn't he have been proud?

Initially, she asked for two weeks with which to submit her resignation to Golden West. Told that even two weeks could make a difference in her seniority list down the road, she was compelled to quit on the spot. She truly regretted having to be a disappointment to the people who had believed in her and opened their cockpits to their first and only woman. "I felt guilty," said Julie, "especially recalling that Abe August had said, 'Now, don't you quit on us!'"

Nonetheless, she resigned from Golden West, an airline that was sorry to lose a good pilot. In stark contrast, the management at National Jet Industries (NJI) was prepared to sue to recover the cost of Julie's jet training when she failed to honor her commitment to the year of flight instructing. "All of a sudden, doors were opening for me. I *had* to go. I settled with NJI out of court, taking out a loan for $5,000 and repaying the loan a few years down the road," she said. "John Mayhew, the man who had told me about NJI, was hired by Hughes Airwest at the same time as I and became a close classmate of mine."

"I was sent to Phoenix, Arizona with Hughes Airwest and felt as if I was on top of the world. I started flying on the F-27, sister ships to the one in which my dad lost his life, and flying with some of the very men who had been co-pilots for my dad. I was flying the line and, although I didn't have my dad's wings to pin on my uniform – they'd been lost in his fatal crash – one of his friends gave me a pair of wings identical to those my dad had worn. I did wear the gold Southwest Airlines wings that my dad had given to me in 1958 when I was just ten years old. For the first year of my hire, I wore them on the inside of my flight jacket and, in that way, Ernie Clark flew with me on every flight."

In an eerie reprise of her father's fatal accident, when Julie faced her first check flight with Check Airman Bill Lovelace, the flight attendant on board happened to be Audrey Andress, the daughter of Ernie Clark's co-pilot Ray Andress. The aircraft in which they were flying was the F-27 2770. Their fathers had died while piloting F-27 2771!

Happy to give up her Los Angeles apartment, Julie rented a room in a home owned by a flight attendant, Pam Flores. She relocated near the Hughes' training site and launched into her new career.

She was hired to fly under the Chief Pilot, Bill Hughes, who was the father of her first love, Ken Hughes. Bill was assigned to Hughes Airwest Headquarters in San Mateo, California. In Phoenix, Chief Pilot Lundgren called the shots. She remembered an early briefing in which Lundgren said, among other things, "'If any of you are involved in an aircraft accident in which there are fatalities and you are at fault, pray that you are one of the fatalities.' I thought, 'That's a horrible thought.' Then he continued, 'And, the best way for you to get off probation is, whenever we pass, I want to have to say, 'Excuse me, who the hell are you?' In other words, stay out of my office, don't get into trouble, just do your job!'"

Julie was the only woman in the room. She recalled, "He looked directly at me and said, 'Julie Clark Ames, that will never happen to you.' I hated being singled out and to have all eyes in the room focus on me. I was the second woman pilot to be hired and the first one hadn't worked out very well. Her attitude had been difficult and she left a bad taste in the mouths of the captains with whom she flew. They weren't about to let me forget it. As the first woman pilot at Golden

West, I'd been treated very well. I missed that friendliness. After I'd been flying for a while, the rumor flew around that stated, 'The first was worst, the next was the best.' But, until I proved myself, my task was made even more difficult. I knew that my probationary period was an even greater test of my ability to fit into the airline. I had to counter the strike that was against me even though it wasn't of my doing.

"Initially, we'd all been hired to train in Boeing 727s as Flight Engineers. When they determined that they didn't need Second Officers, we were all redirected to train as First Officers. In one of the earliest briefings, Lundgren swept his hand to the right and said, 'This half of the class is going to the DC-9.' He swept his hand to the left and said, 'This half of the class – you're going to the F-27.' I was in the left side and I thought to myself, 'Cool.' My dad's fatal flight was in the F-27 Number 2771 and Hughes retained Numbers 2770, 2772, and 2773 on the line."

During Julie's probationary year, she received a note in her mailbox telling her to report to Lundgren's office prior to her next flight. Like a schoolgirl, she felt her stomach contract and took a quick intake of breath. She thought, "What in hell could this be about?"

She reported as requested and the Chief Pilot asked her to close the door. He asked, "You've been flying with two particular captains, is that correct?"

"Yes, sir."

"Have they been treating you well?"

"I wasn't about to say a word against them. I told Lundgren, 'Fine. Good.'

"Are you enjoying the job?"

Julie had a fleeting mental picture of one of Hughes Airwest's bright yellow airplanes, airplanes known affectionately as "Top Banana of the West."

She answered honestly, "I love it. I feel as if I've died and gone to heaven. I feel like I should pay *you* for letting me flying these beautiful yellow airplanes."

"Well, sometimes," he ventured, "those two guys are difficult. They are a little different. You are doing a great job. I just wanted to hear from you how you were getting along."

Julie wanted to say, "They're *psychotic*, not just a little different," but, she said nothing. She discovered later that the reason she was flying with the two so much was because all of the other pilots bid around them and thus they flew with those on reserve. She said, "When you are on reserve, you don't have the luxury of such bidding and you don't dare complain about the captains with whom you fly."

Reason for Complaint

One of the men took to the cockpit of the F-27 with Julie early in her hire. She was far too junior to call him on the carpet and too new to handle his harassment successfully. Until she was off reserve, she never breathed a word about what had been a compromising and dangerous situation.

"At the time smoking was allowed in the cockpit. We had passengers aboard and were flying from Phoenix to Yuma to Blythe to Los Angeles, planning to RON in Santa Maria. We were on takeoff roll and it was my turn at the controls. He lit a big cigar and, when I called, 'Gear up,' he retorted, 'Gear's jammed, can't get it up. Gear's jammed.'

"I turned to him and asked, 'Really?'

"His response was, 'No, but pretend that it is. What are you going to do about it?' I glanced at the emergency procedures, knowing that, with passengers aboard, this was no time for emergency procedure practice. Having committed them to memory, I shot back that we needed to manually raise the gear.

"Then he started blowing smoke in my face. I coughed and asked him what in the hell he thought he was doing. He told me that there was smoke in the cockpit – fire! – and repeated his question, 'What are you going to do about it?'

"I told him that I had to don the oxygen mask and put it on full, 100%.

"He said, 'Then, *do* it.'

"These weren't quick-donning masks like the ones in use today. The masks hung behind us and were full face glass masks tightened with rubber bands. They were heavy and cumbersome and looked for all the world like a fireman's glass shield. It was required that one pilot take the controls while the other got the mask on his or her face. I said, 'Okay. You've got the airplane.'

"He challenged me with, 'I'm incapacitated.'

"I had no idea of the enormity of this at the time. It was happening quickly. I was on probation and on reserve. I felt compelled to do as I was being told. It was harassment, but I strained to follow his directions and simultaneously make sure that the flight was safe and the airplane was being correctly and sanely flown. I was under horrendous pressure. Even though my dad had loved the F-27, I felt that it was underpowered and unstable. I was *struggling*!

"The captain thought the whole scenario was funny while I fought back tears. I couldn't believe that he was doing these things. I hadn't seen the worst, though. He called, 'Gang bar *down*!' Isolate the fire by shutting down the electrical switches.

"The gang bar was intended to rapidly depress all of the switches, simultaneously turning the switches off. It was intended to relieve a pilot of having to shut down one switch after another in the case of an emergency. I, of course, simulated the gang bar down. I couldn't *really* depressurize the aircraft, turn off the radios and all of the rest of the vital electrical system items.

"This was the desert Southwest! Temperatures skyrocket in Tucson and Yuma, Arizona, in the heat of the summer. The air grows turbulent with up and down drafts and here I was being called upon to stabilize the aircraft, simulate the radio call for emergency, request immediate clearance to land in Yuma, and I was still wearing the damn mask. It was sweaty; it was too large. As it slid down my face, I clutched at it to push it up. I was humiliated; I was embarrassed and sweating like a pig. I looked over at the jerk who was giving me such a terrible time and I couldn't fathom what was going on in his warped mind.

"Finally, before touching down, he let me take the mask off. We continued on to Blythe, from there to Los Angeles, and on to Santa Maria. Deplaning took time, so, with all of these stops, it was about 8 o'clock p.m. before we shut the F-27 down for the night.

"*Now*, he wants to go out for drinks, for dinner and *dancing!* I told him, 'No. I'm whipped. I'm going to my hotel room.'

"He said, angrily, 'This is a debriefing and you *will* go out and we *will* debrief this flight.'

"I said, 'Let's debrief in the lobby of the hotel.' But, that wouldn't do. I felt that I had to give in to his demands because, as my captain, he could have reported *anything* back about me. It was a horrible situation. I truly *was* tired and I didn't want to be any closer to this guy than sitting opposite him in the cockpit. Even that had proven to be too close. I finally got through to him that I did NOT want the evening to go on any longer..

"Interestingly, he never pulled such a stunt with me again. When my classmates and I got off probation, Rick and I had a big party. The cake said, 'Congratulations To Us!' and I finally felt as if I could tell my story. One of the men in the training department told me, 'You shouldn't have done what he said. It's abnormal to run emergency procedures with passengers aboard. How unsafe can you get?' But, he understood my position, too. I shouldn't have been *asked* to make the flight unsafe in any way. Luckily, I left Phoenix and never saw that pilot again."

Another Bad Apple

Even though Julie had been to dinner at the home of another captain and his wife and children, cockpits could bring surprises to normally cordial relations. One evening, she was paired with him for a flight that was also in Arizona, but was destined to be flown through a black and violent storm. It was all they could do to maintain attitude while the turbulence tossed them from one altitude to the next.

She said, "Back in F-27 days, you flew *through* the weather. You couldn't get high enough to fly above it. That night we were airborne in horrendous weather and struggling to hand-fly the aircraft to the best of our ability. The old C-band radar was cluttered. We were surrounded by storms. I thought, 'God, We're going to die tonight!'

"He kept yelling, 'Just fly attitude. Just fly attitude!'"

"At any rate, we had a stressful flight and the next morning we were outbound from LAX and headed for Phoenix. As we taxied out, I listened to the Automatic

**Flying the aerobatic Pitts in
Phoenix, Arizona**

Terminal Information Service (ATIS) which stated, 'Advise when Number 1 for departure, Advise you have Kilo.' That had been policy with Golden West and I made the radio transmission, 'Number 1 for departure. Have information Kilo.'

"Well, the captain lost it! He screamed, "You do *NOT* have to tell them we're number one for departure. That is not even a mandatory call. Why in the hell are you doing that?""

"I tried to tell him it was on the ATIS and went to crank up the radio and he slapped my hand. He yelled, 'I don't need to hear it on the ATIS. I'm telling you, you don't need to *do* that.'

"He flipped like a cracker jack. Then he told me, 'Just sit on your hands and look straight ahead. When you talk to me and you look at me, you'd better have a smile on your face. Maybe I'll let you fly today and maybe I won't.'

"Not long afterwards, he calmed down and he reached over to touch me on the shoulder. He apologized, but I couldn't help but think that my probationary year was spent, in part, with a couple of psychopaths. Luckily, there was some great release in aerobatic flying during after hours."

On days that Julie didn't fly, she took to the skies in a short-coupled, agile, little Pitts biplane, an S-2 "two-holer." At Stellar Airpark, she flew Smokey Stover's Pitts. Smokey, a Hughes Airwest DC-9 Captain, was starting an aerobatic school. He generously gave her an hour of practice aerobatic flying for every hour that she instructed. She joined the Phoenix Chapter of the International Aerobatics Club (IAC). More than 50 chapters of the IAC, which is headquartered at Oshkosh, Wisconsin, as a part of the Experimental Aircraft Association (EAA), exist and vary in size and activities depending upon the length of the competitive flying season, the proximity to a designated aerobatic "box" of protected airspace, and the enthusiasm of the organizers and members. Arizona is highly prized for its clear skies, clean air, beautiful mountainous terrain and picturesque valleys. As Julie discovered, the IAC is a lively and enterprising club in Phoenix, in Tucson, and elsewhere in Arizona. That arching dome of blue sky practically demands that pilots soar into it.

The flying was intoxicating. Julie gave up precious moments that she could have spent in Morgan Hill with Rick in order to become a better and more proficient pilot. She admitted, "I started flying a Pitts when I had some free time. I was at fault. Instead of going home like a good wife to Morgan Hill, I stayed in Phoenix and raced out to the field with my aerobatic waiver. I had a ball putting the snappy little Pitts through its paces. It was a challenge and I loved challenge."

After she completed her probation at Hughes in Phoenix, Julie transitioned into the DC-9 in September 1978 and was assigned to San Francisco. She moved back home to Morgan Hill. Maybe now, she and Rick could get their lives on an even keel. Unfortunately, because of a strike by the Hughes Airwest ground handlers, both she and Rick were out of work in 1978.

Competitive flying and rebuilding her T-34 had aroused so great a passion in Julie that it should have been no surprise that she turned to her airplanes when time fell heavy on her hands. Just as, when she was hard to find as a little girl, her parents knew that she'd be perched on a picket fence watching the airplanes at the airport in the valley below, now she disappeared to the intriguing surroundings of fabric, dope, glue, wood, and metal. In the carport and in the hangar, she worked on two huge projects: building a Christen Eagle kit plane and restoring her T-34.

In 1977, she met Frank Christenson, the designer of the small biplane that was built on the design of the Pitts. She bought one of his earliest kits and said, "In our carport, I built the upper and lower wings and I built the tail feathers. I really got involved with it. It was *fun*. Fabric work is fun; you get a tremendous satisfaction from having accomplished the building of a wing – stitching the fabric, painting on the dope, tightening the cover. If you could glue and staple, you could build a Christen Eagle. Frank's instructions were so easy to follow.

"But my purchase of the kit plane was another nail in the coffin of our marriage. Rick thought I was crazy to get so involved in competition aerobatics to the point of building my own airplane. He didn't like flying in a Pitts and he couldn't fathom what it was that attracted me. I sold the project to a mechanic at Hughes Airwest and put my energies to restoring the T-34. That was an airplane that we *had* flown together. Perhaps we might once again.

"All of this change might not have irreparably condemned our marriage. We might have been able to work out our long separations and our conflicts. I'd been away more than I'd been home during my night mail flight time with Golden West and in my quest for more turbojet/turboprop multiengine flight time. Then, during my first probationary year with Hughes, I stayed in Phoenix because I was on probation *and* because I was on reserve. I was on the short leash of reserve for the first five years of my airline career. Similar to a military pilot on alert, any airline pilot on reserve knows to stay within a shouting distance of Ops in case there is a chance to be called to fly. It's called "minimum call out" and I really couldn't commute home nearly often enough."

"Rick was a good person; he stood behind me when I was trying to establish an airline career," Julie said. "We really had a good thing going and I take a lot of the blame because I wasn't there. But, the final nail in the coffin of our marriage started in Phoenix. I received several anonymous letters in my mailbox at operations (Ops). The first one started with, 'Dear Julie Ames, We are a concerned group of flight attendants. This concerns your husband and his involvement with

**Julie brings her T-34 home from Alaska.
An engrossing restoration process begins.**

another flight attendant...'

"I was almost physically sick. I knew that Rick and I had faced difficulties. In Morgan Hill, I shared the letters with Rick's mother. Janet said, 'Let's just keep this quiet, dear. Let's pray about it.'

"When I was transferred to San Francisco, I received a final note from a flight attendant, Gayle , who was one of my dearest friends from our days in Queens, New York, with TWA. Written entirely in Spanish, Gayle repeated the accusations, knowing that Rick was involved with others. It was the final straw.

"When I confronted Rick, he suggested that we could stay married and live as if divorced. I said, 'No way! Absolutely not a chance.' We divided everything up as fairly and amicably as possible and we were divorced in 1979."

Author John Updike wrote that same year, in the foreword to his *Too Far To Go*, "That a marriage ends is less than ideal; but all things end under heaven..."

Julie ended up in a small condo in Livermore after she and Rick split up. The divorce was final in 1980. Four short years of marriage and a lot of frenetic activity had pushed two capable people into their chosen career paths and pulled the same capable people apart.

"Wally's" Restoration

Julie turned her prodigious energies toward the restoration of her T-34A, preparing a record of her airplane's rebirth through restoration. She wrote the following description of all that was entailed in the remarkable transformation of a tarnished metal airplane from Alaska into a highly reflective and beautifully appointed performance and air show craft:

As any aircraft owner knows, aircraft are like children when it comes to expenses, i.e., the feeding (fuel and oil), clothing (paint and polish), shoes (tires), housing (hangars or tie-downs), schooling (licenses and insurance), medical and dental treatments (maintenance), and all the other care and loving attention they get from proud parents. This is the Baby Book of my T-34. "Wally."

Every airplane should have a name.

As a proud mother who has worked hard to take care of "Wally," I would like to share some of the moments captured on film. Like many baby books, this contains a lot of firsts: "Wally's" first hangar, new paint, new looks, new tires, etc. Please indulge me as I show off my T-34 from Day 1 in Anchorage, Alaska when I first took delivery of "Wally," purchased sight unseen, to the day he rejoined the military, resplendent in his silver and blue, Julie's version of the "Air Force One paint scheme."

Rebuilding an aircraft is a huge job, even for the experienced. Julie did much of the work herself.

The Initial T-34 Restoration, 1979-1980.

For a period of 8 weeks I borrowed a friend's hangar, put the airplane on jacks, and with the help of another T-34 owner, tore down my airplane for its annual inspection. Then I proceeded to continue into a major project of refurbishing the entire interior that had seen no attention in 25 years.

The following – a real learning experience – are the major items either improved upon or replaced:

Detailed wheel wells, i.e., sandblasted, cleaned, and painted.
Main gear doors, painted
New wing landing light lenses, installed
Stripped rubber and painted along wing chord
Added military placards to exterior fuselage
Stripped, cleaned, sanded, and painted aft baggage compartment
    and entire interior of the front and aft cockpits
Repainted and placarded front and aft cockpit instrument panels
Selected and supervised painting of wings and fuselage in style of
    military Air Force One, i.e., lettering, military stars and bars
Front and aft cockpit mirrors, installed
Cut and fit rubber matting for baggage area and cockpit floors
Removed both canopies and cleaned both canopy rails
Changed N number from N1405Z to N34JA
Installed front cockpit glare shield

The T-34 "Wally," Rebirth, Renewal, and Restoration

In April of 1977, I read an ad in *Trade-A-Plane* for a sealed bid on a Civil Air Patrol T-34 in Anchorage, Alaska. Having received my commercial certificate in a Navy T-34B in 1976, I knew I would love to own that type of airplane. After receiving notice from Anchorage that I'd won the bid, I flew to Anchorage on a commercial airline and, sight unseen, picked up the airplane I had just bought.

Due to my new job at Golden West Airlines, I had only two days to fly 2,900 miles from Anchorage to Los Angeles. "Wally" and I arrived in Hawthorne, California, tired and dirty; but, that trip was the start of a continuing love affair between "Wally" and me. We hit all the air shows in the Spring of 1978, but didn't win any judging contests. "Wally" still looked like an Air Force reject. My campaign to restore and renew the plane started that Fall.

My ideas for a new paint job, radio gear, and replacement of the magnesium surfaced flaps had to be carefully budgeted. The seats were original including the complete survival kits beneath the cushions and sitting on canned beef, signal mirrors, and emergency flares is anything but comfortable. I had an IFR package installed to replace the one Com/Nav (communication and navigation radio) and then commenced work on the exterior.

In one tragic/comic moment, after two days of prep, systems cleaning, sanding, and painting, I installed a nose gear assembly with an added aluminum placard. I crawled back to the aft fuselage tail compartment via the baggage access to clean and found the true meaning of weight and balance. My weight upset "Wally's" balance while on wheel jacks. We both survived.

Using drawings, I designed and color-coordinated the racy paint scheme that fits "Wally's" lines, yet didn't look too civilian or too military. Aero Design in Healdsburg did the actual painting while I looked over their shoulders every step of the way. I wanted enough polished aluminum to look good, but not under the

A prize-winning Air Show Airplane

wings and belly as buffing those is a terrible job and it's hard enough to keep up a gleam on the body and upper wing surfaces.

Once "Wally" was out of the paint shop, I had to polish all the aluminum by hand. Anyone who has done it will tell you, this is a definite labor of love.

I selected the material and form for new seats so that they would fit the new paint scheme, be easy to clean, and long lasting. They were sewn by a friend of mine in Arizona. The instrument panels were next on my list and were double the trouble and double the expense. This Spring, 1979, we again hit all the air shows and fly ins from California to Arizona. "Wally" dazzles one and all as he proudly gleams on static display. His new engine and prop have given him new life and together we enjoy flying even more, if that's possible.

A famous photograph of Julie in her Mopar T-34
by Michael Haberlin

"Wally" and I are a team. "Wally's" restoration included:

Rebuilt engine O-470-13A
New custom designed paint
New propeller, very difficult to locate
Gear doors added
Replaced magnesium flaps for aluminum
Replaced augmenter tubes
IFR package installed
Acid-etched interior engine cowling and painted
Completely hand-polished the exterior
Installed canopy cover snaps

Was Ray Andrews naming the aircraft or naming the pilot when, in 1978, he wrote on the T-34, "Free Spirit?" It is descriptive of both.

In one special and serendipitous moment, Julie discovered words written beneath "Wally's" skin by unknown persons who also loved and cared for this particular T-34A. Having removed all of the inspection plates for the annual inspection, Julie found the following:

"This aircraft has served well. We hope it will end up in good hands and never in the junk pile after leaving Air Force Command duty. Spence Air Base, Georgia, 1961."

It is almost as if you can hear "Wally" replying,
"Thanks, guys. I found a good woman.
You should see me now!"

Fokker F.27
"Friendship"

CHAPTER TEN: *LOGBOOKS DON'T TELL ALL*

Responsibility hangs heavily on the shoulders of a flight instructor whenever someone she has taught to fly runs into trouble or, worse yet, is killed at the controls of an aircraft. One flight instructor lost two former students and could comfort herself only knowing both of them were killed outside of the envelope of the lessons she had tried to instill. There is no way to teach good judgment. Aviators have to take the best instructors offer, but judgment develops from their beliefs, their character traits, their intelligence, their knowledge.and, when they are accrued, their experiences.

In one case, a flight student, in his mid-sixties, was delighted to learn to fly. He took some aerobatic lessons from another instructor before taking off in a normally-aspirated single-engine trainer aircraft from a high altitude mountain strip in Oregon. Before reaching 50 *feet*, he attempted to roll the aircraft. His judgment was disastrous; the crash, fatal.

Julie faced tragedies that took the lives of three significant men in her life. She had flown with each of

Tony Olivera and Julie

them, of course; but, she was not to blame for their errors in choices, their experience levels, and the particular circumstances that proved their undoing. Nonetheless, the pain is excruciating.

Tony

After her divorce, Julie threw herself with even greater intensity into her other passion – her airplanes. She said, "I was flying for the airlines and, for a time when I'd just checked out in the DC-9 and was based in San Francisco, I was on reserve and I didn't fly a whole lot. Sometimes I called just to make sure I still had a job. They didn't have an overwhelming need for pilots, so I had a lot of time to work on the airplane I owned."

When polishing her T-34 in front of her hangar one day, she and Tony Olivera got acquainted; the attraction was immediate and it was strong. Julie was rebounding from her divorce from Rick and she fell deeply in love. Tony, who with his parents owned Olivera Farms, a chicken ranch in Los Banos, California, was the father of three children and, at the time, was separated from his wife. As entranced with flying as Julie, Tony owned his own aircraft, a Beech Bonanza A36, and flew to and from a strip on his ranch.

As Air-Marking Chairman of the Golden West Chapter of The Ninety-Nines, Julie had participated in the painting of a compass rose on the strip. The newspaper write-up stated,

> "The Olivera Farm airmarking was 13 and 14 October 1979. Organized
> by Julie Clark Ames, Helen Kelton, Bay City 99s, did the Technical
> Direction, and many Golden West 99s and guests contributed work. The
> hard workers were kept replenished with sandwiches and cold drinks and
> entertainment provided by Tony Olivera and Julie Ames in a fun air show.
> Tony Olivera is the young man who treated the 32 workers to a fantastic
> dinner at the Flying Lady Restaurant. After a heavy day of airmarking on
> Saturday, Julie and Penny Becker went back to the ranch on Sunday. The
> dynamic duo painted Golden West 99s on the taxiway. Tony Olivera super-
> vised and okayed the job as the sun set."

Julie and Tony had flown to and from the strip several times, picking up veterinarian medicines, flying to and from other air strips, and, in their own airplanes, practicing formation flying – skilled flying Julie perfected at NAS Lemoore and shared with him.

"He was a good formation pilot. He'd tuck the airplane in so tightly and stay right on the wing. Sometimes I had to tell him to back off a little.

"I was so in love with him. We hit it off from the moment we met and we had so much fun together. He had a great sense of humor and everyone who met him thought a lot of him.

"I'd only known him seven months before he was killed. It was a horrible accident. We'd made plans to fly to Morgan Hill to meet another couple for dinner. Tony and I took off and he got into position on my wing.

"We'd often flown together and sometimes we teased one another. Sometimes he'd get on my tail and we'd do "tail chases" all the way back to Morgan Hill. Sometimes we'd change positions from one wing to the other, or drop back out of sight, or pull up and away. His airplane was faster than mine, so he sometimes zoomed ahead. At any rate, one moment he was flying on my wing and the next, he was *gone!*

"I called on the radio, 'Come on, Tony. We have friends waiting for us. We don't have time to mess around. Where *are* you?' But there was no response. I thought maybe he had pushed the throttle and charged ahead of me. I flew on into Morgan Hill and asked my friends, 'Is Tony here? Have you *seen* him?' When they told me they hadn't, I dashed back to my airplane. While I was firing up to go back to Los Banos, the police called to tell my friends not to let me fly, to keep me on the ground because there had been a crash and a man had been killed.

"When I got back to Olivera Farms and saw the fire burning on the ground, it was just four miles off the end of his airstrip. I landed and took one look at the faces of his employees and knew the awful truth. Tony had crashed! Tony was in that fireball! I was hysterical! It was 26 May 1980. He was only 29 years old! He had everything to live for! He *couldn't* be dead!

"Representatives of the FAA interviewed me. Then, Wally Funk, tested as an astronaut with NASA's Mercury Program and an Accident Investigator, also tried to shed light on the horrible crash. She helped me to deal with the awful reality, although I was so shaken, I could scarcely think. I told Wally he hadn't radioed me, hadn't complained of anything going wrong. He never said a word. He simply disappeared from my wing. Wally and the other members of the National Transportation Safety Board (NTSB) found nothing wrong with the aircraft mechanically. There was no *reason* for him to end up crashing and auguring into the ground. The anguish was so much greater than I could stand. I was crushed. Completely devastated."

Julie retreated into herself. She didn't eat; she didn't sleep. She called Hughes Airwest to tell them her boyfriend had been killed on Memorial Day weekend and that she didn't know when she would be able to come back to work.

Several days later, the doorbell rang and she opened it to find her Chief Pilot, Bill Hughes, on the doorstep. She tried to shut the door before he could come in.

"Captain Hughes had driven all the way from San Francisco International Airport to my home – a distance of 70 miles! It was a huge step for a Chief Pilot to take and I appreciated it; but, I didn't want to see him and I didn't want him to see me. I had surrounded myself with cards that Tony had given to me, articles about Tony, and pictures – lots of pictures. I didn't want Captain Hughes to see the state that I was in.

"He pushed his way in and spent the day with me. He told me 'You've got to quit this! You've got to pull yourself together. You have everything going for you. This is a *chapter*. It is tragic. I'm sorry for you, for what happened to your mother, to your dad, and to your boyfriend; but, damn it, you've worked hard for this job and I worked hard to help you get this job.'

"If it hadn't been for Bill Hughes, I don't know what would have happened to me. He was so strong. He saved me from God knows what. I couldn't face the truth. I was at one of the lowest ebbs of my life.

"Bill put it in perspective for me. He said, 'You have to mourn; but, you have to carry on.' I couldn't even think like that."

Not long after Tony's fatal crash, the Morgan Hill Airport closed and Julie not only was coming to grips with her grief over Tony, but she was thrown into turmoil about relocating and finding a hangar in which she could store her airplane. She made a move to a condominium in the Livermore Pleasanton area when she found a hangar at the Livermore Airport. The move was beneficial and the timing was good.

Mike

Mike Van Wagenen and Julie dated during 1981 and 1982, having met at air shows held at various sites around California. Prior to excelling as an air show pilot, Mike made a name for himself as a very bright Air Force pilot, a fighter pilot who served during the Vietnam conflict. On the air show circuit, Mike flew a Pitts biplane in an act with Vern Dallman called *Me and My Shadow*. Later, he performed with a three-ship team, the *Sierra Aces*.

Mike was a good looking guy and Julie enjoyed being with him and being with the other performers on the air show circuit who welcomed her into their midst. She was new and, in her characteristic way, she was carrying the load of two full occupations – her airline piloting and her efforts to create an air show persona. She and Mike were intimate for a time, but when it became obvious their relationship wasn't going anywhere, they parted. They remained close friends.

Mike Van Wagenen and Julie

Mike became president and test pilot for Peregrine Flight International in Minden, Nevada, throwing his energies into the BD-10 program. The BD-10, a Jim Bede design, made a debut in 1989 as a two-place, very high performance, single engine jet aircraft intended to be the first homebuilt kit jet and purported to achieve speeds of 900 mph to Mach 1. Its characteristics were impressive – from brake release at Mojave to 10,000 feet in 46 seconds and Mike often urged Julie to invest in what he believed in so strongly. In truth, there was no dearth of persons willing to invest in a speedy jet able to be created as a homebuilt. Mike intended to use the BD-10 as his sleek steed on the air show scene. Tragically, on 30 December 1994, he was at the controls when the tail of the jet failed structurally and took another exceptional pilot to his death.

Julie said, "It was awful. Just tragic. He had so much to offer."

Gary

Julie first met Gary Loundagin, a mechanical engineer, in the late 1970s – just as she was becoming interested in performing in air shows and after she purchased her T-34 and was hard at work in its restoration. In a scene eerily reminiscent of her first meeting with Tony Olivera, Gary saw her polishing her airplane on the tarmac at Livermore Airport in 1981 and introduced himself once more. After telling Julie he had purchased a T-34 located in Vermont, he asked if she would travel east with him to pick the craft up and to fly it back to California.

"He told me, 'You're a flight instructor, so you could help me master the craft

Gary Loundagin and
his T-34 named, "Truly Julie."

on the return flight. Also, you're with the airlines, so you can travel back there for minimal cost.'

"The two of us flew commercial airlines back East and picked up his Mentor. I had to get back to work and, as I was based in Las Vegas, I dropped him off in Salt Lake City, Utah, with the explanation, 'Gary, you're doing fine. You don't need my help any more and I need to get back to work.'

"It wasn't long, however, before he was reportedly buzzing runways and generally flying recklessly. He seemed to push his envelope, testing his limits, and getting himself into situations that got out of hand quite quickly. Nonetheless, primarily because of our shared interest in T-34s, we started dating in 1982. I think, in part, I pitied Gary, a concern which slowly grew to a fondness. We became engaged in 1984."

Cameron Park, California

By happenstance, while seeking a small pump for her smoke system, Julie met with fellow air show pilot, Chuck Lischer in Cameron Park, California – one of the first times she had visited the residential airpark. While there, she discovered a house was for sale. "It had been a repo," she said, "a spec home built by Earl Ancker whose buyer backed out of the deal. It wasn't quite completed, but I wanted to buy it. I asked Earl to include an attached hangar and Gary and I decided to share in the purchase of the home. We shook hands on it all around."

There were complications, as there are in most relationships. Gary was divorced from his wife, who had moved to the East Coast, and their teenagers remained in Livermore. Julie said, "It wasn't easy for him to keep two homes going; it strained his disposition, too. He could be a volatile and aggressive man. He let his ego invade his capability. After I sold my home in Livermore and moved up to Cameron Park, I discovered I was losing any passion I had felt for him. Love was growing cold and I was filled with regret that we'd purchased the home together.

"Fortunately, Gary had kept his home in Livermore and was willing to have me buy him out of the Cameron Park home. Fortunately, too, I could afford it."

Then, fate intervened. Gary suggested that he and Julie perform a two-ship act. He seemed to resent any success she enjoyed and pushed himself to perform beyond his capabilities. When she insisted they remain solo performers, he accepted an invitation to perform at the Mammoth Lakes Airport, California. An air show novice, this was his second air show appearance and he chose an airport located at an exceedingly high altitude.

At an airport elevation of 7,128 feet above mean sea level (MSL), a performance in Mammoth's mountainous terrain meant flying the traffic pattern at an altitude of 8,000 feet. In the summer, the factors of altitude, temperature, and humidity combined to challenge even the most proficient of pilots operating normally aspirated single-engine aircraft. All high altitude airports are placarded with the warning: *Beware High Density Altitude* and letting pilots assess the results of flying in areas of high temperatures, high altitudes (with less air density), and high humidity. When it's "High, Hot, and Humid," an aircraft operating at 8,000 feet might perform as if flying at 12,000 feet or above. *High Density Altitude* has everything to do with aircraft performance. Julie said, "It is like flying your airplane at half power."

Prior to the air show, Julie tried in vain to dissuade Gary from performing at Mammoth. To this date, she has set a maximum of 5,500 feet as the field level from which she'll fly. Operations in and out of a high altitude airport during normal air traffic operations on a hot, turbulent summer day were a challenge. Accepting a slot during an air show added the pressure of performance to already high-strung competitive zeal. It was a recipe for disaster. In attempting to perform so high, he was overextending his own capabilities and those of his aircraft.

As Gary took to the skies near the majestic Sierra peaks, Julie was performing at the Petaluma Municipal Airport, Sonoma County, California. In dramatic contrast to the demands upon Gary's piloting skills, she was flying off of pavement located on the valley floor at 87 feet above sea level. She and her airplane were operating at a pattern altitude of less than 1,000 feet. Her normally-aspirated engine could develop full power.

Her crew chief, Larry Littlepage, interrupted Julie after her act while she was signing autographs. Larry told her, "They called your name over the P.A. system, Julie. You have a telephone call."

Julie said, "Russ Francis, well-known as a tight end for the San Francisco

49ers and familiar pilot at the National Championship Air Races, was on the telephone. Russ generally flew at Stead Field, Nevada, in a P-51 Mustang. *What on earth can he be calling me about?* I wondered.

"Russ said, 'I'm sorry to be the one to tell you this, but Gary just went in with his T-34.'

"I was stunned. 'Went *in*? Is he dead?'

"'Oh, yes,' Russ answered.

"I offered the phone to Larry. 'Would you take this?' Larry got all the particulars and I told the organizers I had to leave the air show. I was madder than hell. I was sad. I was torn and I was shaken.

"Later, when Larry and I watched the video of the accident, his second maneuver was a loop. The ground just came up to meet him. He did an accelerated stall, pancaked in, and broke virtually all the bones in his body. It was 1986 and he was only 42 years old!"

Julie felt responsible for retrieving Gary's body and his belongings. The next morning, she wheeled a Cessna 310 from a friend, promising to fly it carefully and well and cherishing the experience of her days with Agri-Till. She flew to Mammoth Lakes, near Mammoth Mountain and in the shadow of the towering 14,000-foot Eastern Sierras that pierce the blue sky like so many saw-teeth. Willows and cottonwood trees hinted of underground water sources and the rich scent of chaparral, pine, and fir wafted around her as she stood next to the airplane waiting for the ambulance. If her heart hadn't been so heavy, the beauty would have held her in its grasp.

"Gary's airplane hit so hard that it stayed intact, although the engine and the propeller flew off. He'd crashed alongside the runway, smacking sharply into the gravel. The canopy sprung off except for its center section. When they picked up one wing, the fuselage was supported. I was amazed at the strength of the T-34. When they removed the airplane, its outline was preserved in the gravel as if a huge cookie cutter had stamped the shape in granular dough. The airplane dispersed the gravel completely in an abrupt stop. It was eerie.

"They provided me with a blanket with which to cover him and helped me put him into the plane. It was awful; it was a dreadful moment."

Julie was the executor of Gary's estate. She made arrangements for the casket, the funeral, the delivery of Gary's body to its burial site in Waitesburg, Washington. Later, she had a headstone created in Minneapolis and shipped to Waitesburg. She was the instructor who had signed Gary off, had checked him out in the airplane, and taught him aerobatics. When she finally broke down, she sobbed, filled with remorse over the fact that someone to whom she'd been a mentor was dead in an accident embodying the antithesis of all that she had tried to instill.

The late Bill Hughes

"I taught him everything and he still killed himself! It brought back all the torment of having lost Tony Olivera. The anguish was unbearable.

A Coda

"One of my friends put both of his hands on my shoulders, locked his eyes on mine and said, 'You can teach a pilot to make a good landing. You can teach a pilot to make a crosswind approach. You can teach to the best of your ability, but you can't teach judgment, Julie. You will have to let go and not carry this guilt.'

"I so wanted the message to reach into the painful, emotional bonds in which I was gripped.

"I hope sometime I can help someone who is so deeply in mourning. I have been so blessed to have good friends help me. You *have* to get on with your life. You *must* take it as one chapter. I'd been in dreamland, but I couldn't dream on, I had to *carry* on.

"I was so appreciative of Bill Hughes telling me, 'You take all the time you want; but, trust me, I'm going to call you every day. I'm going to make sure you are pulling out of this tailspin because you are going to hit the ground unless you do something positive with yourself.'

"He followed through. He called me every day and, finally, I told him I was ready to come back to work. He arranged for me to check in at a certain time and to take just one short out-and-back trip. I went out to do the walk around on the DC-9 and I remembered that I'd taken Tony on a couple of flights. Back then, you could take a friend on the ramp. Tony would buy a ticket and fly with me to Seattle or Portland and return. He said then, 'I want to do a walk around with you. I want you to show me everything you know about this airplane.' He was so into what I was doing.

"I was doing the walk-around and I started crying again. Bill came out and I said, "I just don't know if I can do this.' He called a reserve pilot and I went home. I carried on, finally; but, it was a week before I could do so. I would be happy to be the same tower of strength to someone else who is in mourning that Bill Hughes was for me."

The Mopar T-34 in its 2004 paint scheme

CHAPTER ELEVEN: A KALEIDOSCOPE OF COLOR

As her career in the airlines progressed from having been a hostess with TWA, a flight attendant with Universal and with World Airways, to conquering the cockpit and flying with Golden West, Hughes Airwest, Republic Airlines, and ultimately Northwest Airlines, Julie's uniforms and the aircraft paint schemes, their livery, illustrated the many changes she underwent and the colors painting her life.

As a flight attendant with TWA and World, she represented the era in which hostesses were hired as stylish, perky beauties, selected on their obvious physical attributes and having passed demanding standards of excellence. That she had been the beautiful Homecoming Queen and Miss San Carlos fit into this picture; that she could speak fluent Spanish certainly meant she was an excellent choice for European routes.

When she was hired as a pilot by Golden West Airlines, she flew as first officer on aircraft bedecked in the reddish gold of the rising sun with compass roses decorating the tails. Having submitted applications to virtually as many airlines as existed in the mid-1970s, she received word simultaneously from two before she had completed her probationary period.

The Red of Northwest

"I sent out a ton of applications," she said. "United, Delta, Allegheny, Mohawk, American, Continental, Western, and, of course, my dad's airline that had become Air West and then Hughes Airwest."

It could never have occurred to Julie at the time that her life would be composed of a series of mergers and choreographed in bright colors of various liveries, new and different uniforms, aircraft purchased for one airline and absorbed by another, with complex seniority lists bearing their own kaleidoscope of color. She never could have imagined the "Green Overcast" until she lived to see it.

When her father flew for Pacific Air Lines, the F-27A wore bold red-orange stripes. They swept from below the sleek black nose, back across the door and over the eleven rounded passenger windows to a swoosh at the tail. Emblazoned on the rear fuselage was an emblem of a spread-winged eagle boasting the airline's name. By 1 July 1968, Pacific Air Lines had ceased to exist. Like a whale ingesting smaller fish, Air West, with its vivid two-tone painted tails rising from stark white fuselages, emerged the victor.

By August 1972, eccentric multimillionaire Howard Hughes purchased Air West and titled the airline with his name – Hughes Airwest. Headquartered in San Francisco, the airline underwent a design makeover and resulted in sun-splashed yellow from nose to tail of the airliners and bedecked the flight attendants in brilliant yellow outfits. Promotional ads screamed, "Top Banana of the West," and the distinctive flying fruits became familiar at airports from Great Falls, Montana to Astoria, Oregon and from Seattle, Washington, to San Diego, California and Tucson, Arizona. Although Howard Hughes' death in 1976 preceded Julie's hire by a year, his airline boasted a fleet of 49 jets when Julie came aboard.

"I was on probation for a full two years," Julie explained, "first with Golden West and then with Hughes Airwest. With Hughes, I was domiciled first in Phoenix and then in San Francisco.

"I only flew for Hughes for three years, which was really an amazing chapter in my life – it was so special to fly the airplanes Ernie Clark had flown and with the crew members Ernie Clark had known. By the time I was flying with them, the rule requiring cockpit doors to be locked was called the Clark Act and stemmed directly from my dad's fatal flight. By then it had been determined that Ernie Clark and Raymond Andress were the first in history to be killed at the controls of an airliner and everyone aboard the aircraft was condemned to the same fate.

"Yet, on one truly memorable flight, Gene Malm, who had been a pilot with Pacific and had known my dad, was in the Pilot In Command (PIC) position – the left seat – on one of my flights. As I settled into the right seat, Gene said to me, 'I have something for you. I'd like you to have these.'

"He reached into his pocket and handed me a set of Pacific Air Lines' wings. I never had my dad's wings except for the gold wings from Southwest. I gasped! All I could say was, 'Oh, my God! How can I ever thank you?' They formed a start to my collection of wings and are a compilation of my dad's airline and military wings and my own airline wings and my affiliation wings. I have a one-year pin with Hughes Airwest, a five-year pin with Republic, and a ten-, fifteen-, and twenty-year pin from Northwest. I ended my career with my twenty-five-year pin.

"I loved flying with Hughes. I loved what we flew; I loved where I was based. Life was good. It was simple. It was so easy then."

As Julie had flown as First Officer to Gene Malm, who had flown as co-pilot to Ernie Clark, Gene's son, Eric Malm, flew as a first officer in the MD-80 with Julie as his captain. The story came full circle.

In 1980, her probationary period over and her position as a successful air crew member secured, Hughes Airwest was sold to Republic Airlines. Republic, in turn, had resulted from a consolidation one scant year before of North Central Airlines, which had begun as Wisconsin Central in 1946, and Southern Airways. Julie changed uniforms once again.

She said, "When I went from first officer in the MD-80 out of Las Vegas to captain on the Convair 580 in Minneapolis, I turned back forty years in technology. When you are checked out on new equipment, you are 'frozen' on that equipment so the airline isn't constantly facing the costs of retraining. Our freezes then were nine months. At the time, I said, 'Man, I'm outta here in nine months. I'm outta here.' Cold? Flying in the middle of winter? We flew at altitudes between 18 and 25,000 feet. We never flew above the weather. We flew *in* it. That airplane was *cold!* I'd never flown in winter snowstorms. We were flying in the Upper Peninsula of Michigan. It was the most challenging year of my career. It snowed every day. We flew from Minneapolis to Duluth to Sault Ste Marie, Houghton Hancock, down to Traverse City and into Detroit. There we spent the night and then made the return flight the next day. It was *cold*. But, it was flying at its best. I thought I'd leave the Convair after nine months. I ended up staying for 4 ½ years! It was great! It was valuable experience. When we parked the Convair 580s in November of 1988, I was #1 captain on the seniority list.

"I was also one of the few, I imagine, who ever rolled a Convair 580! Sent to Hibbing, Minnesota to fly a requalification check, which at the time could not be flown in a simulator, I took off with a check pilot. He and I were alone in the aircraft and, after we completed the check, the pilot asked, 'Ever rolled this thing?' Of course I hadn't, but the idea was intriguing. I was game! We requested a 10,000-foot block of airspace, briefed carefully and, with the check pilot handling the thrust levers, I pulled the nose over the horizon. What a blast! We not only rolled once, we made six or seven rolls, improving with each one. Months later, having to fly another requalification ride, I went to Rochester and happened to be assigned to the same check pilot. This time, however, we had another pilot undergoing the check with us. He took to the controls first and, when it was my turn to be tested, the first pilot went to the galley for a drink of soda. This time I was asked, 'Remember how to roll this thing?' We briefed carefully once again, arranged for the block of altitude, and up and over we went. We were leveling off when the first pilot came charging into the cockpit, went to his knees, and gasped, 'I thought we lost it! I thought we lost it!' For some of us it was more fun than for others But, I recognized that I hadn't been exhibiting my best judgment."

Merger Chaos

Flying could be fun; but, mergers were painful. To illustrate their complexity, Julie recalled, "North Central, headquartered in Minnesota, merged with Southern Airways one year prior to merging with Hughes Airwest. North Central and Southern became Republic. When Hughes Airwest was taken into the mix, we became a big domestic airline and were based in Minneapolis."

Not only did the aircraft paint schemes change to a dramatic turquoise swoosh from black nose to tail, but the representative design of a flying duck (nicknamed "Herman") slicing through a hoop was emblazoned on the tails. The logo was carried on as Republic's logo – had been in effect since 1947. The uniforms changed several times.

"I called it a three way merger, even though it took over a year for the three airlines to come together," said Julie. "From 1980 to 1986 life was okay. The seniority lists were finally organized, we went through umpteen paint jobs, umpteen presidents, and we were finally getting a good structure. A three-way airline coming together with three different operations offers a bumpy road to an employee. Sometimes you'd get on an airplane still painted yellow, but Howard Hughes' initials (three diamonds) were gone. Perhaps "Herman" would be painted on the tail or airplanes hadn't been painted or a logo hadn't been established. Sometimes you'd wonder, 'Where'd this plane come from? Where are we going? Are we a day late or are we about right on time?' We received paperwork via teletype and it could be confusing. Crewmembers didn't merge for a long time and the first time we did, flight attendants came aboard wearing different uniforms. 'Wow. How come you are wearing blue shirts?' It took a while for cohesiveness to come together. Yet, if I thought the seniority problem in the Republic merger was tough, I hadn't seen anything yet."

In 1982, Julie upgraded to First Officer, Republic Airlines MD-80 / DC-9. Then, in 1983, she had her first opportunity to bid for a captain slot. Several months later, she became one of only a few women who had achieved this coveted position in U.S. Airlines. Prior to 1982, Denise Blankinship and Maggie Rose became Captains with Piedmont; Sharyn Emminger was named Captain with Hawaiian, and Nancy Keith Johnson wore Captain's stripes for Federal Express. In 1982, four women became Captains: Helene de Saint Genois, Air Trans; Gloria LaRoche, Interstate; Lynn Rippelmeyer, People Express; and Sheffie Worboys, Evergreen. In 1983, Emily Warner, who had earlier become a Captain in de Havilland Twin Otters, was named by the International Society of Women Airline Pilots, as having become a Captain for Frontier Airlines. She was joined by Lennie Sorenson, Continental, and Meg Ann Streeter, Evergreen. Julie's promotion to Captain in 1984 with Andrea Rice, Hawaiian, meant she was among the first dozen women pilots to be so elevated. It was the goal toward which all airline pilots aimed and a crowning achievement for Julie.

Majors, Nationals, or Regionals

According to R.E.G. Davies, "In October 1980, the C.A.B. recognized the inevitable. Effective on 1 January 1981 all U.S. scheduled passenger airlines were redesignated either Majors, Nationals, or Regionals, based on a qualifying level of $1 billion annual revenue for the Majors and $75 million for the Nationals. The decision was a direct consequence of the epoch-making legislation, under the Carter Administration: the Airline Deregulation Act of 1978."

Republic Airlines, which was born after the Airline Deregulation Act of 1978, was elevated to Major status. When Julie underwent the merger from Hughes Airwest to Republic, 14,800 employees had to be integrated from one company to the next.

"The seniority question is always a big deal," said Julie, "but the merger from Hughes to Republic wasn't nearly as bad as the 23 January 1986 transition from Republic to Northwest."

Although the merger madness represented a feeding frenzy, a commonality among the three airlines with which Julie flew was the operation of MD-80 / DC-9s. Republic Airlines served 107 cities with a fleet of 168 aircraft and maintained hubs at Minneapolis, Minnesota; Detroit, Michigan; and Memphis, Tennessee.

Deregulation offered its own brand of confusion, opening a plethora of instances of intense competition. Entering into more than a year of negotiations, the presidents of Northwest Airlines and Republic eventually agreed to a purchase. For $884 million, Northwest bought the assets of Republic Airlines in October 1986 and was suddenly the fourth largest U.S. airline, having jumped from seventh place. Julie flew DC-9s painted in sun-bright yellow, DC-9s bearing the flying duck ("Herman"), and DC-9s with the distinctive red tails of Northwest Airlines.

Of the merger, she said, "Adding our employees of Republic to those of Northwest went on for three or four years. Some delegate based in Hawaii was paid a lot of money by the Air Line Pilots Association (ALPA) for his crafting of one list from the two. One of the results of the merger for me was to keep me in the DC-9.

"With my time in service, I ought to have upgraded into a DC-10 or a Boeing-747. We called it the "Green Overcast" because our seniority number rushed us directly to the top – *years* later – when we upgraded to bigger equipment from which we had previously been restricted. We Republic pilots were designated Green Book and Northwest pilots were Red Book. The color differentiation came from the color of the contract book cover. They will *still* sometimes ask whether a pilot is Red Book or Green Book.

"Our contracts back in the early days of Hughes were able to be slipped into the breast pocket of our jackets or shirts. Today's contracts are written by attorneys and seem to be aimed directly *at* attorneys. The contracts are so thick they are kept in binders and are regularly updated with revision papers. They were made for lawyers, period. If a pilot has a grievance today, he or she would have to go to the local ALPA attorney to decipher the contract.

"Our contracts used to be written in normal language, like the Living Bible, you could understand it. Luckily, my seniority has meant I didn't even have to call scheduling. I was senior, I got my schedules, I flew my trips, did my job, completed my revisions, took my check rides and my physicals, and I went home.

"I did have one interesting encounter in 1986, just after the merger. I met a

147

Northwest woman pilot in the elevator in Memphis. We were in the midst of the horrendous merger that dragged on for years and tempers were frayed. She introduced herself, then she said, after a few amenities, 'All I can say is you'd better not end up being senior to me.'

"I asked, 'When were you hired?'

"She said, 'I was hired in 1979.'

"'Well, I was hired in 1977. May the best man win.'

"'It's been a pleasure to meet you,' the elevator door opened, I walked out."

Not all altercations were unpleasant. She explained, "Not too long ago, I was walking down the concourse and someone kicked at my bag, piggy-backing on my roller case. I turned around with a dirty look and found Will Tannahill, now a retired chief pilot. He grinned and said, 'You need a new bag.'

"I told him my bag had to last until retirement. It was my original Hughes Airwest bag and, scruffy or not, I wanted it to last for my whole airline career. I did have the inside rebuilt – books were pulling it apart. But, Will wanted it to be clean and new-looking.

"I teased, 'Since when does a flight bag change how you fly your airplane?'

"Will was cool with my comment. He laughed."

At one time, it was possible for newly hired pilots to become captains within five years. The larger the airline grows, however, the longer it takes to upgrade. As mergers occur, seniority numbers continue to shift *against* advancement. Julie said, "If you start with 1,200 pilots worldwide, then have 2,400 pilots, then 4,800, and now on up to 6,500, seniority lists get mangled. Merging three lists exactly by date of hire and time in service is the way it should be, but it's not the reality.

"The merger for Northwest included numerous restrictions known as a 'fence agreement.' A decision limited Green Book pilots to get on widebody jets as Green Book pilots retired or as new aircraft were purchased for the fleet. The merger occurred in 1986 and this fence won't drop until 2006. That's the length of an entire career.

"It seemed over the years that every time my seniority neared 1,000, I had 999 pilots senior to me and 5,500 pilots junior to me. Having endured as many mergers as I have, when my number approached 1,000, it meant we were going to merge!

"When I approached 1,000 at Hughes, we merged three ways with Republic with a total of 2,400 pilots. For the next six years, I worked my way down from 2,200 to close to 1,000. We merged and poof – my number went way back up to 3,000 plus. The numbers are reevaluated every January and every July. It was only with Northwest that my seniority number broke 1,000 and we didn't merge. Mergers are very hard on individual pilots, but they make the airline strong, large, and competitive."

"Pilot of Disabled Jet Believed to be a Woman!"

En route between Las Vegas and Baton Rouge, Louisiana, in 1983, Julie was First Officer in a Republic MD-80 that blew a tire on takeoff. The eruption sounded like an explosive blast! Julie didn't realize at the time that the ghastly hole blown through the flap on the right wing – three feet in diameter – was clearly evident to passengers on the right side.

She said, "My twin sister, Judy, was pregnant with my niece, Heather, and I remember that it flashed through my head, 'I might never have a chance to see her!' It was a frightening experience.

"The day was blistering hot – 110 degrees. The aircraft was at max gross weight with a full load of passengers. The tire, a retread, shredded. We were doing a zero-flap takeoff because of the temperature, the high density altitude, and the weight. We hated that kind of takeoff because at times those tires spun up to 150 knots. The retread snapped off and up through the retracted flap and into the engine.

"I glanced over at the captain and he seemed paralyzed.

"I said, 'Sir, we just lost the right engine.' He hesitated.

"I asked, 'Positive Rate?' as a trigger to alert the Captain. We had to focus on procedures.

"He said, 'Uh, …gear up.'

"'Let's clean it up,' I said, as we attempted to climb above Las Vegas' surrounding mountains. I radioed to declare what had happened while the engine went through a compressor stall. The chunk of tire was eating through the engine like a corn cob and causing a dreadful banging and clattering. Tower operators called to tell us they'd not only gathered a pile of rubber from the ground, but they'd gathered a pile of metal as well.

I responded, 'That's probably the engine.'

"The tower controller asked, 'What's your state of affairs? How many souls on board? What's your fuel state? Then they started to tell us to enter a holding pattern.

I responded, 'Sir, could you just get us vectors and headings?'

Everything was up to the decisions of the captain; but, I was trying to run the checklists, trying to declare the Mayday, trying to talk to the flight attendants who were knocking on the door. The screams of passengers could be heard through the cockpit door. It was just awful.

"We told the controllers to prepare for our landing and requested that the ARFF (Air Rescue Fire Fighting) be standing by. We couldn't return and land immediately because we were well over our landing weight. There was no capability to dump fuel from the MD-80, so, we circled, assessing what we *didn't* have. Even then, we landed overweight.

"One flight attendant came forward, sweating from the heat. We'd had to turn off the air conditioning packs. We didn't want to overboost the only engine left. It was sweltering throughout the airplane, but we couldn't help it. We had no air!

"In fact, we didn't have much. We lost everything on the right side – hydraulics, brakes, flaps, all our fluid. We knew we could get the gear down, but knew it would be at a much slower rate. We didn't have any anti-skid, nor did we have reverse thrust on the right side. Complicating all of this was our very heavy weight.

"When we finally landed, the captain did a good job. We didn't go off the end of the runway, although we used up every inch of it. We didn't taxi in – we were towed to the gate. Simultaneously, helicopters landed with members of the press aboard. I had to lean out of my window to make a request of a ground operator and the next day's paper screamed, 'Pilot of Disabled Jet Believed to be a Woman.' To them it was more newsworthy than that we'd just landed successfully and all of the 143 people were safe."

Were women pilots never to be fully accepted? When Julie was a new hire with Hughes Airwest, the press arrived, drawn by a whiff of the newsworthy item. She needed to use a bathroom and walked down a long hall in Seattle, Washington, only to be followed by pushy reporters with microphones and cameras. One of them yelled, 'There she is!'

Julie said, "I ran into the bathroom and tried to stay there long enough for them to become discouraged. When I finally came out, they surrounded me, their notebooks out and ready. I was furious. I just wanted to be treated normally and to do my job.

"Fortunately, the Chief Pilot Bill Harris told the press to back off, to let me be. I just wanted to fly my trips and be an airline pilot! I hated such press coverage."

Ever vigilant, the press never relented. In the winter of 1985, Julie flew as captain on a Convair 580 and lost an engine. Electing to divert to Bismarck, North Dakota, it was another of the north's snowy, blustery, windy, ugly nights. She said, "I had a strong crosswind into the side of the dead engine. The correction I had to make was *against* the dead engine. I was worried that I couldn't hold the airplane on the runway after landing.

"It took a lot of rudder pressure; but, I kept it on, stopped in plenty of time, and faced the press after the incident was over. I was on television, shown telling reporters it was 'just a routine landing.' Our Chief Pilot in Minneapolis, Sarge Martin, called me at my hotel room. 'Captain Clark? Sarge Martin here. So, to you that's called a routine normal landing?'

"I had tried to downplay the whole event a little bit. Sarge continued, 'I just

151

want to say, 'You did a great job! Come see me tomorrow when you get in.'

"It's gratifying when you receive kudos!"

Networking

Julie joined ISA +21 – then the International Social Affiliation of Women Airline Pilots – as one of its 21 charter members. The founders chose an acronym symbolizing the group and commonly used among aviators. To ISA – the International Standard Atmosphere – was added the numerical 21 for twenty-one degrees above standard and also counted the original charter members. Julie networked with her sister airline pilots whenever her schedule permitted and she enjoyed sharing some of the humor and some of the pain of their first years. She discovered through her affiliation with ISA +21, her date of hire placed her as the 13th U.S. woman hired as an airline pilot in the modern, scheduled airline fleet.

Interestingly, Jean Haley of San Mateo, California, was president of ISA +21 in 1980. She was quoted as having said, at the annual convention in Denver, Colorado that year, "My father was a crop duster. He was killed five years ago dusting a field. He never lived to see me fly a commercial airliner. He'd be so proud."

Julie had much in common with Jean Haley. Ernie Clark never knew his daughter was even interested in obtaining a pilot certificate. He didn't live to see her take a first flight in a small Cessna trainer nor did he live to see her pilot the very aircraft he piloted as an airline captain. Like Jean Haley's father, however, he would have been so very proud.

A Juggling Act

Julie started on her simultaneous career path as an air show performer in 1980, the same tumultuous year Hughes Airwest merged with Republic. From her home in Livermore, California, she completed the restoration of her T-34 and capitalized on having launched an air show career with two other T-34 drivers. She flew as Colonel Julie Clark Ames with Colonel Dick Tews and Colonel Ed

Messick, all respected member of the then-Confederate Air Force, which has since undergone a name change to the Commemorative Air Force.

Proud to have restored her T-34, she was appreciative of having learned to fly formation at Navy Lemoore and under the guidance of Tews and Messick. The trio formed a three-ship team, the CAF Falcons. Dick Tews painted his T-34 with the logo of Anheuser Busch, his

Julie flew renowned Voyager pilot, Jeana Yeager

sponsor, and called his airplane the "Flying Beer Can." Julie's airplane, whose patriotic paint scheme emulated Air Force One, was also referred to as "Free Spirit" or as "Air Force One-Half."

Because the T-34 lacks an inverted fuel system, any sustained inverted flight is impossible. The three pilots were arduous in their practice of close formation flight, showing their aircraft to their best in aerial choreography that emphasized graceful, fluid maneuvers and maneuvering within inches of one another's wingtips.

In 1985, when the business aspect of creating an air show persona was at its height, she owed thanks to Sarge Martin, Republic's Chief Pilot. Sarge allowed for her to have a leave of absence for the entire summer. It was without pay, but it gave her the unique chance to concentrate on her T-34 and her second career. Her American Aerobatics started its takeoff run.

As Julie's air show reputation grew, she was questioned about her simultaneous career by other airline pilots. She said, "When I won the Art Scholl Award, a press release was submitted to Northwest and published in *Northwest Passages,* the

Julie and her beloved dog "Mags"

airline's magazine that reaches 55,000 employees. I tried to keep my air show business low key; yet, some have challenged my flying for hire other than for my airline. Airline pilots are limited to flying no more than 1,000 hours per year. The airline, the airline pilots' union, and the Federal Aviation Administration all establish
the guidelines by which we fly. However, the flying for hire rule applies solely to
being hired to carry passengers.

"In 1987, I was in the jumpseat in the cockpit of a DC-10 going to an air
show in Arizona. I was headed for a performance in Prescott at Embry Riddle
Aeronautical University and we were also in the midst of the merger from
Republic to Northwest. When one of the pilots recognized me, I told them my
airplane was already in Prescott and I was on my way to an air show. The First
Officer was really rude. He asked, 'How do you get away with doing aerobatic flying and flying for the airlines, too?'

"I said, 'I'm not 'getting away' with anything. What do you mean?'

"He said, 'We're not supposed to fly on the side.'

"'I've never heard that. I've been doing this now for six or seven years and it hasn't been a problem.'

He kept at it. 'I thought we weren't supposed to fly for hire. Aren't you paid?'

"'Yeah, I'm paid.'

"'Then what you're doing is illegal. When this merger is all done, you'll be put out of business.'

"'I hate to tell you this, but I fly under Part 91.'

"'Then, how can you be paid?'

"'You have to have a commercial pilot's license to fly air shows, but I am not carrying passengers for hire. I'm not flying air ambulance or running a charter service under Part 135. *That* would be illegal.'

"To the First Officer, the Captain interjected, 'Why don't you just drop it.'

Maintaining the tight schedules of airline piloting and air show performance proved a juggling act Julie Clark was happy to make. Never easy, however, were the logistics of maneuvering her T-34 from one air show to another. She might have performed in Toronto, Canada on a Saturday, parked her aircraft long enough to get a jump seat aboard an airliner to arrive in Minneapolis, Minnesota, in time for a scheduled airline flight on Monday morning, and then returned to pick up her T-34 and have ferried it to be positioned for the next air show performance in Dayton, Ohio, for the following weekend. She scheduled her airline flights and her air show performances accordingly, but weather-related factors played a part in ferrying her airplane. She said, "I was especially challenged to fly my T-34 through Montana and Wyoming if deadlines pressed and icy, blowing snow, and low visibilities intervened. My T-34 lacks an oxygen system, so the mountain states present problems if I'm forced to climb to higher altitudes for terrain clearance in inclement weather. My airplane is range limited and, of necessity, there are fewer airports in rural areas.

"In 1988, I purchased a home on Sky Harbor Airpark, Webster, Minnesota, 35 miles south of Minneapolis and St. Paul. The appeal of having a centrally-located position for my show airplane near my airline base made the decision for me. Jerry Van Grunsven, a former Hughes Airwest Captain with whom I flew on the F-27 in Phoenix lived on the airpark with his wife, Judy. They were great friends, inviting me and my crew to stay in their home during the summer of 1987. I learned to love the location."

Her home, a pre-fabricated house built in 1975, is situated on a 2800-foot grass runway. Larry Littlepage, her crew chief throughout the 1980s, helped her paint the house, get a hangar rebuilt in which to accommodate her airplane, and enabled her to move into the home in 1989.

Julie has criss-crossed the country to fly between 18 and 20 air shows each season – air shows that are held in *all* of the United States and throughout Canada. At this writing, her T-34 has 12,000 flight hours on the airframe. Her airline career takes her out of Lindbergh Terminal in the International Airport of Minneapolis-St. Paul and requires traveling from her home in California or from whatever location in which she finds herself at the end of an air show performance. She often has to "dead-head" or request a jumpseat on her own or another airline in order to maintain her schedule, a juggling act that would have exhausted an ordinary mortal. Julie has continued to face the challenge with remarkable, accident-free flight hours in her two careers.

In an effort to ensure that one didn't conflict with the other, she kept up with her air show circuit by turning down opportunities to bid for larger aircraft or for international routes. With her time in service, she could easily have been upgraded to the impressive Boeing 747 and have been regularly flying between the west coast of the United States to airports in Japan, Alaska, Hong Kong, and Singapore. Those exotic ports took a back seat to American Aerobatics, Incorporated.

CHAPTER TWELVE: *SKY HIGH*

Tennessee Ernie Ford is the announcer giving Julie a hug when she flew with the CAF

When Julie started flying in air shows in 1980 with the Commemorative Air Force CAF Falcons, there was little organizational skill needed to make arrangements for performances. Although she was proud to be in the first group to have a woman pilot in CAF and the first to be sworn in as CAF Colonel, the air show business was essentially casual at best. She and her crew chief, Larry Littlepage, weren't introduced to the concept of uniforms, photographs, or press releases. Julie didn't have a secretary; she handled all of the business requirements herself. Her airplane was flyable, but it had not yet felt her efforts toward meticulous restoration. If either Ed Messick or Dick Tews heard of an upcoming air show, he might call to ask whether she was available for the date. If Julie knew of a show, she might telephone or hand-write notes to air show organizers to obtain a booking. Payment was rare and gradually came in the form of fuel for the airplane and a free ticket for entrance to the show. Waivers had to be obtained thirty days in advance of the show, flight practice had to be arranged, choreography was necessary and, hence, some forethought was required. However, the loose management of her start in air shows was a far cry from the highly sophisticated business that has evolved.

CAF Falcons, 1983

Julie became a Life Member of the Commemorative [Confederate] Air Force and flew with the Falcons whenever the schedules of two or three of the pilots permitted. The juggling act was already in place in her life and was equally a force in the lives of Tews and Messick, making practices sporadic at best. When Julie entertained the thought of quitting the trio and going on alone, Messick was openly skeptical. He seriously doubted she could make a go of a solo act in a T-34 and his voice betrayed his misgivings when he shrugged and said, "You want to go solo? Lots of luck!"

She was appreciative of the experience she had gained in the tight formation flying with the CAF Falcons, but she yearned to prove herself on her own. She admitted, recently, "I can't name the last time an air show organizer asked me what my act is about. That is nice, but it took a long time and a lot of effort to get to the point my performances are known and recognized."

Now her website – http://www.americanaerobatics.com – proudly announces:

The Mopar Parts T-34 demands tremendous skill to fly aerobatics, requiring great pilot co-ordination and anticipation. Julie's aerobatic routine is truly remarkable in its beauty and splendor. More remarkable is the elegance she exhibits in an airplane whose flying manners could best be described as rugged. Her unique presentation of "Serenade in

Red, White and Blue" with a special added patriotic tribute is breath-takingly choreographed to Lee Greenwood's *God Bless the USA* or *God Bless You Canada*. Multi-colored wing-tip smoke paints her route of flight in the sky throughout the graceful routine, which ends with daz-zling fireworks finale. Her graceful aerial ballet stirs the hearts of young and old alike.

Her detractors have to eat crow and admit, "You've come a long way!"

A Star is Created

With the help of her tax accountant, Harriet Fox, Julie started as a small business in 1980, making the necessary submissions and soliciting under the name Julie Clark's American Aerobatics. Julie painstakingly completed all of the exterior renovation of her T-34 by 1980 and in 1981 she gutted the interior completely and restored it to air show perfection. In 1980, she flew her first solo act at the Merced, California, Antique Aircraft Fly-In. With further assistance from Harriet Fox, she actually incorporated in 1989. Fox encouraged Julie to drop her name from the business so she would be protected as an entity. She was headed sky high!

Getting T-34 Owners Organized

While she was preparing for her solo act and her air show business, Julie also served as a member of the Board of Directors for the T-34 Association. The Board was formed in 1983 and currently boasts approximately 500 members. Among others, Julie joined Lou Drendel, aviation artist and head of the Lima Lima Squadron of T-34s, Jim and Jud Nogle, and their father Charlie Nogle, the aviation professional who formed the association. Nogle's knowledge and involvement with T-34s has spanned 50 years. The board members have carried their passion for their sturdy, single-engine airplanes into virtually every facet of their lives.

The board was responsible, in part, for the handbook on formation flying that has become the "Gospel for Formation Flying" at the annual Experimental Aircraft Association AirVenture at Wittman Airfield, Oshkosh, Wisconsin. Barring 1999, Julie has performed there annually with her T-34 and with the new addition to her hangar, her bright yellow T-28 Trojan, her own yellow "Top Banana." She is a valued member of the Warbirds, a division of the EAA. She takes seriously the importance of the safety of formation flying and the safety of the nearly one million spectators who congregate at Oshkosh each year.

"We flew so badly one year, Tom Poberezny, EAA President, a twenty five year veteran of air shows as a Christen Eagle pilot who teamed with the late Charlie Hillard and with Gene Soucy, and a U.S. Champion in competitive aerobatics, told us, 'If you T-34s don't get together, we don't want you here.' That mobilized us to come up with the guidelines and to perfect our formations. Lou Drendel did all the illustrations for the manual and I was right in there as I'd been doing formation flying since 1975. It is a skill you have to continue to hone. It is an entirely different type of flying; it requires total concentration. If you even start *thinking* about something else, you are out of position. As I said in the Navy, 'You put your wing on the star and shut up. Keep that guy's helmet interlocked with your helmet. Stay *with* it.'"

Focusing on safety and successful formation flying, Julie worked with the other members of the T-34 Association and participated in developing what has become known as F.A.S.T. In order to fly formation at FAA-Sanctioned events under waivered airspace, Wingmen and Leaders must pass a flight test. A pilot must fly wing for a year prior to testing as lead. The F.A.S.T. acronym stands for Formation And Safety Team. John Harrison wrote the following Foreword to the F.A.S.T. Practical Test Guide in 1994:

> In aviation, each rating, certificate, or flying privilege requires the pilot or applicant to demonstrate his knowledge and skill in performance measured against a minimum standard. Each module of performance or individual task usually is demonstrated by a "level of accomplishment."

Each task and the associated level of accomplishment (L.O.A.) are criteria by which an evaluator is able to judge and measure an individual's depth of knowledge and his / her ability to perform to a minimum standard.

In all instances in which aviation knowledge and skill are required, the individual must have taken a "check ride" to demonstrate competence. A check ride or flight test is the aviation community's way of providing for an evaluation of an individual's total knowledge and the ability to maneuver an aircraft precisely according to demands of the rating. Regardless of the rating or certificate, the process is the same.

The flight test process ... [is divided into] modules or tasks that usually incorporate tolerances in levels of performance. While we are all familiar with the average stated standards of heading (+ / - 10°) or altitude (+ / - 100') for general flying, no such criteria has been developed for the civilian evaluation process to judge the quality of formation flying on an individual task basis, objectively!!!

The emerging National Formation Policy Committee, by definition and intent, is promoting a standard. This organization has officially adopted the curriculum of the T-34 Association *Formation Flight Manual* and Darton International's *Formation Flying, The Art* video. The syllabus of each curriculum is dedicated to the basics of formation flight. Each of these teaching aids, the manual and the video, is integral to the process of safe formation flight, the manual for describing the standards, and the video for teaching and visually demonstrating the process.

However, neither the manual nor the video has standardized or codified the valuation process. Concomitant with the National Formation Policy Committee's goals of standardization in formation flight as it relates to all of the U.S. Warbird Community, we are establishing a flight test process that incorporates criteria for evaluation. This criteria has been developed for each maneuver and is organized as an objective flight test guide to be used by each formation check pilot.

The current valuation process as specified by the T-34 Association manual provides for formation pilot certification by "…performance and maneuvers to a [level] acceptable to the check pilot." This subjectivity is desirable in a small organization where like aircraft are all being flown. Merging all Warbird organizations in the process of standardizing formation flight demands more structure. The primary emphasis of new structure is a standardization of check pilots from all organization through the use of annual meetings and a "standards of performance" manual or flight test guide for formation pilot wingmen and leaders.

It is recognized that the flight leader is the cornerstone of the F.A.S.T. formation program. Therefore, the selection, training, recommendation, and evaluation of new flight leaders should be held to the highest standards. Furthermore, standardization is the key to having a successful national formation program and every attempt must be made to ensure that standard practices are followed in the selection, training, and evaluating of flight leader candidates.

Julie is proud of her commitment to safe flying and to having been recognized as a leader in the skills of formation flying. She is qualified as wing and leader in both the T-34 and in the T-28 and she is proudest of the statement made to her immediately after a qualifying wing check ride for another formation pilot. Julie closed in steadily and Check Airman Jim O'Neal, at the end of the flight, said, "I've got a new name for you. When I looked at you, you were always where you were supposed to be. I'm going to call you 'Glue.'"

Her accomplishment, as in all facets of aviation, cannot afford to be neglected. Like any other athletic skill, formation flying requires dedication, rehearsal, and repetition on the part of the pilot who risks his or her own life and the lives of others if skill levels are allowed to get rusty.

American Aerobatics, Incorporated

Once the incorporation was completed, how did Julie obtain sponsorship and product support? She said, "I am indebted to a lot of people, but I especially thank Bobby Bishop and the late T.J. Brown for their help. Bobby was flying the Coors Silver Bullet and I admired his act as well as the man. He told me: (1) I had to demonstrate an impeccable safety record and an impeccable personal record. When sponsors consider someone to represent their company, they investigate your past, checking for criminal records and every other item that might prove an embarrassment were it to surface. (2) I had to come up with an image to target the market needs of the company. (3) I wasn't to put all my eggs into one basket.

"I went through magazine after magazine checking advertisements. I thought, with my red, white, and blue patriotic theme, I was a natural for Chevrolet. I could envision myself in their ads: The 'heartbeat of America,' for instance, would play directly into the heart that I create in the sky with smoke.

"I spent a year chasing Chevrolet, but was rejected at every juncture. I created presentations, made hundreds of telephone calls, even borrowed a computer to create some of the publicity ideas that came to me and to write some of the hundreds of letters I wrote.

"Finally, a friend suggested I try Chrysler, now DaimlerChrysler, believing Lee Iacocca was certainly avant-garde and doing productive and innovative things. I had admired Lee Iacocca, had purchased his autographed book and learned from some of his ideas. I wanted to look at my business as he did. He said, 'In the end, all business operations can be reduced to three words: people, product, and profits.' I took that to heart and, when someone told me, 'Don't write. Call someone in marketing,' I placed calls to Chrysler.

"I managed to connect and was told, 'We aren't currently interested in such a sponsorship, but why don't you call our division of Mopar? They might be interested.'

"I contacted a friend, a graphic illustrator, Chris Ceccarelli, and asked him if he knew anything about Mopar. He told me about Mopar and about Chrysler, Dodge, Plymouth, Jeep, Eagle, and Dodge Trucks – the "Six Pack." He talked about Muscle Cars of the 70s. I had some homework to do."

After some research, Julie discovered Mopar had extensive experience in motor sports and performance vehicles. She organized her intentions and, 1987, called. Told, "We're budgeted out until 1992," she was persistent. She reorganized her promotional material, having Chris help her with art work, and called again. This time she spoke with Mr. Jerry Blake, Mopar Parts Marketing Manager. He invited her to make the first of her presentations. Elated to be getting her foot into the door, she flew to Michigan and made her way to the Centerline, Michigan, offices of Mopar Parts.

"I talked with Jim Nogle when Jerry Blake asked for a 'letter of intent.' Jim told me to put one together in bullet form and to use a fax machine to send it off. I knew from my experience at American Airlines that getting in the door was the hardest part. I had to demonstrate a wholesome and an appealing representation; I had to demonstrate I could lure customers. I also had to show I was willing to go more than half-way to meet their product support needs."

Finding sponsorship was far from easy. Mopar wanted to know how many media impressions she could demonstrate, what radio and television affiliates had carried information about her, whether some of her coverage had been live, pretaped, or edited; where she would be seen, by how many she would be seen, and

164

what her needs might be.

"It was daunting," admitted Julie. "I had to dedicate myself to showing the people of Mopar that I fit into their niche and would attract people to their products. Like Iacocca said, it was 'people and products.' Now the 'profits' part was up to me.

"I was so excited! I promised them I would never let them down. When they suggested having to paint my airplane, I went so far as to return to California to remove a panel of the highly-polished aluminum and to return with it to Michigan in order to show them exactly what the airplane looked like. Photographs weren't enough. I felt very fortunate that they changed their minds about the painting and we were able to come to an amicable agreement that has lasted throughout the years.

"I was ecstatic to receive a contract for two years from Mr. Blake. Since then, the contract has been renewed annually and I am dedicated to enhancing the image of Mopar and drawing as much attention to Mopar Parts as possible. I've been fortunate to have been included in auto racing events that draw national attention to racing and have even flown the legendary 'Big Daddy' Don Garlits onto Bandimere Raceway in Morrison, Colorado when he was honored as the Grand Marshall of the Mopar Parts Mile-High National. Auto racing events have been as much fun for me as some of the aviation events. To say I'm indebted to Mopar for the support I have received over the years is a masterpiece of understatement."

Having spent twenty-four seasons as an air show pilot, the 2003 air show season marked the sixteenth year Julie has been honored to having been sponsored by Mopar of DaimlerChrysler. No other solo performer has held a professional relationship with the same corporate sponsor and the same airplane for this length of time. Obtaining sponsorship has been an ongoing task and Julie is to be commended for her obvious capability in returning to her sponsors and to those who offer product support for her special brand of attention and marketing skills. She constantly has their names and logos before the crowds and ceaselessly draws attention to them. She also never fails to recognize and offer appreciation for their generosity.

In addition to the essential and inestimable value she receives from DaimlerChrysler Mopar Parts, she receives product support from Victor Aviation Engines; Bendix /King Avionics; Bose Corporation Aviation Headsets; Concorde Aircraft Battery Corporation; Goodrich Weather Mapping Systems; ICOM America, Inc.; Champion Spark Plugs; Softies-Paraphernalia Parachute System; Pulselight Landing Light Systems; GEM Insight – Graphic Engine Monitoring System; GAMIjectors – Aircraft Engine Fuel Injectors; Flight Guide Publications; Phillips 66 Aviation Lubricants; Air Chart Systems; Tilley Endurables, Inc.; American Propeller Service and Eagle Engines; Goodyear Aviation Tires; Sandel Avionics, Inc.; Shadin Aircraft Fuel Management Systems; Voo Doo Wax; and DuPont.

Several crewmembers have maintained and negotiated the long cross-country ground support necessary to a successful business and, to maintain an orderly and organized headquarters, Julie has hired excellent assistants. Operating from the office building behind Julie's home and hangar are those talented women who have been essential to the running of her American Aerobatics. For six years, C.J. Freeland was indispensable, as is Misti Flaspohler, a pilot and a good friend who has been with Julie for four years and currently provides the essential continuity in maintaining an active office and a flourishing business.

Julie's typical air show schedule gives an indication of the distances she must fly to get her airplanes on site and the distances crewmembers must drive to get her support vehicles to the same sites. In 2003, she performed in the following states and provinces and in some multiple times: Manitoba, British Columbia, and Ontario, Canada; in the western United States in California, Washington, and Wyoming; in the central states of North and South Dakota, Ohio, Michigan, Missouri, Wisconsin, Tennessee, and Texas; and in the eastern United States of Florida and Connecticut.

Imagine the logistics of ensuring such a schedule! She has to negotiate the arrivals and departures of one performer, one or possibly two airplanes, costumes, wingtip smoke canisters, fuel requirements, a truck, promotional materials, specialty fireworks products, and the myriad of accoutrements of a crew, and has, in addition, the incredible demands of having a full career as an airline pilot. Julie is to be commended for her incredible energy, her dedication to her chosen path, and her persistence in seeing that both of her careers were juggled successfully. The challenges are staggering. For her airline career, her travel from her home in Cameron Park, California, to her second home in Minneapolis, Minnesota, placed a burden of commuting on an already heavily pressured pilot. Her website states:

"While Julie personally ferries the Mopar Parts T-34 to each air show, her ground crew travels an average of 30,000 miles per year. The Mopar Parts T-34 Team's ground support "Road Show" includes a custom 35-foot Featherlite, triple axle, 5th wheel trailer with living quarters up front and storage in the back. The pulling power needed for the unit is supplied by a 1998, Cummins Turbo Diesel powered, Dodge Ram 3500 Quad Cab pickup. The Cummins Turbo Diesel torque peaks at 440 LB-ft, with manual transmission – the highest diesel torque rating available in a light-duty pickup. The 5th wheel trailer carries all necessary support materials and serves as day quarters during air shows. The custom décor features a trailer that has been "wrapped" with decals that depict Julie's Mopar T-34 in flight with Julie in her flight suit with fireworks in the background. The complete unit is displayed on the air show flightline, providing a focal point to meet the public, sign autographs, and display Mopar materials; it can serve as a base for local Chrysler dealers to display their cars. Julie and her crew can also be seen with the 'Road Show' at a variety of Chrysler Corporation dealers on their aerobatic tour. 'I am proud to be carrying the Mopar Quality name into the skies,' says Julie, 'and we provide even greater exposure for Mopar on the highways and on the flightline.'

"Clark's graceful aerial ballet is a symbol of pride and patriotism. A pilot for more than 30 years and a Captain with Northwest Airlines, Julie has logged more than 27,000 accident-free hours in the air and is rated in more than 65 types of aircraft. With a personality that shines as brightly as "Free Spirit," her restored Mopar T-34, Julie takes the Mopar T-34 to the limits of its operating capability as she entertains millions of people annually, averaging 18 to 20 shows each year. She has appeared in the biggest air shows in the United States, Canada, and Bermuda and, in 2004, she intends to perform in the contiguous United States as well as Canada, Hawaii, Mexico, and Alaska."

An Award Winner

Julie has performed for tens of thousands of fans in her twenty-five seasons as an air show pilot. She has earned the admiration of fans and fellow performers and she has been the recipient of a long list of awards and honors. In December 1998, Julie received the prestigious Art Scholl Memorial Showmanship award during the 30th Annual International Council of Air Shows Convention ceremonies in Las Vegas, Nevada. This prized award is presented annually to the air show performer who best exemplifies Art Scholl's commitment as an entertainer. The Scholl Award is an ultimate award for air show stars and Julie felt awed and honored to be considered among the best performers in the industry.

In 1981, Julie was the youngest recipient of the "Woman Pilot of the Year Award," given by the Southwest Section of The Ninety-Nines, a woman pilot organization formed in 1929 and presided over initially by President Amelia Earhart.

In 1988 and again in 1997, *General Aviation News* named her "Performer of the Year" and, in 1988, 1990, 1992, and 1997, "Favorite Female Performer." Julie, whose dedication to aviation caused her to be called a legend in her own time, has been given a Certificate of Appreciation by the FAA in Washington, DC, for: "Outstanding Contribution to Professional Women in Aviation," "Contribution to the Preservation of Military Aircraft," and, with an award that has only been presented six times in the last decade, "Contribution to Women Pioneers in Aviation." Nominated by Jim Schram, a Northwest Airlines employee, Julie was inducted into the Pioneer Hall of Fame by Women In Aviation, International in 2002.

Her fellow air show pilots selected her to be the recipient of the 1991 Bill Barber Award for Showmanship. Dave Weiman, Publisher and Editor of *World Air Show News*, said, "Through a combination of pilot skill, imagination, personality, attitude, and a style all her own, Julie Clark displays the qualities of a true showman and projects a positive image of the professional air show performer."

In 1993, she was inducted into the Forest of Friendship in Amelia Earhart's hometown of Atchison, Kansas. She saw to it, later, that her father, Ernie Clark, receive the same

Julie and her sister, Sharon, take to the T-28 to enshrine their father in the Forest of Friendship.

prestigious honor. Her sister, Sharon, joined her for the touching enshrinement of their father in 1999.

An animal lover, Julie rarely flew without her beloved dog, Magneto, "Mags." Julie was a captain on a Republic Convair 580 one snowy, blustery early spring morning in 1985. She discovered a frightened, abandoned puppy at a Holiday Inn in International Falls, Minnesota, captured the pup, and smuggled her aboard the Convair for the trip home. "Mags," an appealing Terrier mix, was Julie's companion for 16 years. Like the air show dog she was, she wore a puppy flight jacket and scarf and traveled happily in the T-34. Featured on the "Mack & Mutley" show and on "Prime Time Pets," she caught the eye of Joan Rivers, who hosted Julie and Mags on "The Joan Rivers Show."

Although there is no replacement for "Mags," Julie now owns two dogs –

Mollie, a Yorkshire Terrier; Bernie, a Lhasa Apso – and a small parrot, a Green Cheeked Conure named Ernie in honor of her dad that was given to her by famed aerobatic champion and air show star Patty Wagstaff.

Featured on many nationally televised television documentaries and aviation-related programs, she co-hosted the "P.M. Magazine's Sky Dancers" special and appeared in the PBS specials, "Reaching for the Skies" and "The Adventurers". She was also featured on "The Dayton International Air Show Television Special" in which she gave Robin Leach, of "Lifestyles of the Rich and Famous," his intro-duction to aerobatics. Julie's expertise and love for aerobatics drew the attention of "ABC's Wide World of Flying" and she appeared on "To Tell the Truth." Julie was interviewed on the Discovery Channel for a documentary entitled "Inside the Black Box," which delved into the technology that has occurred in commercial aviation since her dad's fatality and the fatalities of 11 September 2001.

Perhaps as a result of some of Julie's publicity, in 2003 she received a message from Wayne Brander, a General Sales Manager of Reno Jeep Chrysler in Nevada. He wrote, "My father was a passenger on flight 773 in 1964. Only recently did I learn that your dad was the pilot. I'm sorry for your loss." Julie knows they share an irreparable tragedy.

When asked to tell her most memorable flying experience, Julie recalled the flight in which she gave then-Chrysler President Bob Lutz a ride in her Mopar T-34. He was the number one person at Chrysler and he was a former U.S. Marine Corps pilot. She said, "He had me do aerobatics over the Chrysler proving grounds with a lot of people watching from the ground knowing Mr. Lutz was in the back seat." The second was flying as a passenger with Canadian Snowbirds for their full air show. That ride was a never-to-be-forgotten, once-in-a-lifetime delight. Finally, she recalled having narrowly escaped a disaster early in her flying career. In 1984, she was doing a four-point roll and her seat separated from the runners and slid all the way back to the stops. Barely able to right the airplane and narrowly missing a tree, she immediately landed, shaken, but miraculously unhurt. Larry Littlepage bolted the seat in place and there it remains secured.

Safety First

Julie has been gratified to have been accident free in the air. She said, "The only thing I've ever dented was an MD-80, while parking at Detroit Airport in 1991. It was a snowy night and I had my eyes on the marshallers who were guiding me to a parking place. There are clear zones and cones that mark the spots at this time. There was apparently a deicing truck on my left side and it was beyond my view. My job was to focus on the marshaller and we were to watch for his or her signals. The marshaller, on the other hand, was supposed to monitor the wingtips and the wingwalkers to give a thumbs-up as they guide us in.

"All of a sudden, we felt a lurch. I thought it was the jetway, but we weren't in a position to have the jetway come toward us yet. I saw him form the word 'F...' and I thought, 'Uh oh. What's going on?'

"I'd struck the deicing truck. I didn't get into trouble, but I had to go through the report process. It hurt the wingtip, breaking the plastic assembly in which the strobe, the navigation light is housed. I never heard another word about it.

"Later, the marshaller wrote in the accident report, 'I looked up at the pilot and fixated on the fact that she was a blond.' He was fired.

God Bless the U.S.A.

In defense of the man, he wasn't the first or the last to be entranced to see a beautiful woman at the controls. Many fans react the same way when they see the diminutive blond stand up out of the cockpit at the end of her performance, her arms spread wide holding the striped and starred American flag for all to see.

Even Lee Greenwood, to whose beautifully patriotic song she flies, wrote, "We all dream of flying. As a young boy, I used to dream that I could fly without an airplane. I still have that dream occasionally. Because Julie Clark flies with my song 'God Bless The USA,' I feel with her in the cockpit. Her safe flying record and patriotic display is a credit to her personally, and to the American Woman."

**Julie's T-28 Trojan is painted bright yellow
and named "Top Banana" in honor of
Hughes Airwest,
"Top Banana of the West."**

CHAPTER THIRTEEN: *A MISTAKE, NOT TOO LATE*

A Beautiful Bride,

There is a unique vulnerability in Julie Clark. Despite having suffered the losses of her parents, men to whom she was engaged to be married, boyfriends who might have become paramount in her life, and many friends who have loved aviation as much as she, she repeatedly has reached out with trust and without guile. At the same time, she has created her own business, conducted herself in highly competitive fields of endeavor, and has successfully assumed a highly professional and rigorous role as an airline captain in what still remains as a 'man's domain. She embodies the qualities of these complex differences. She has the naïve trust of one who gives of herself generously and the steely resolve of one who has become accomplished in leadership positions. These complex traits are admirable; but, they have caused her more heartache than she deserves.

Having been featured prominently in many magazine articles, Julie's fame has spread and she has become well-known and highly-respected for the flair of her showmanship as a performer and for her business acumen in launching and maintaining a successful business. Perhaps publicity has two faces. Reputability is essential to foster a business. Julie needed all the positive publicity she could get; it fed her air show persona. Conversely, the fame and notoriety invited the unscrupulous to her with the tenacity of drones attracted to a queen bee. As many who become famous can attest, they are surrounded by flattery. Insincerity is one of the more difficult traits to recognize. Sometimes it masks scheming. Sometimes it is recognized too late.

In 1991, in one of the high points of her career, Julie was brought forward on the stage at the world's largest air show, the EAA Convention and Fly-In in Oshkosh, Wisconsin. There Dave Weiman, Publisher and Editor of *World Air Show News*, honored her with the coveted Bill Barber Award for Showmanship. She exulted in one of her happiest moments.

By the end of 1991, at one of the lowest points of her life, Julie was faced with defending herself in divorce proceedings brought upon her by the plaintiff. Fortunately for her, the judge recognized the seriousness of the charges, understood she had been swindled by one of the slickest con men in California, and found her without fault. Rather than opt for a divorce, he granted her an annulment. She had grown accustomed to dealing with "chapters" in her life and, with a hearty slam and a "Thank GOD! I'm FREE!" she closed this depressing chapter.

Tip of the Iceberg
It all began innocently enough when Penny Becker invited Julie to a Super

Bowl Party. The new year of 1988 was newly started and Julie, who had seen to Gary Loundagin's burial the previous May, hadn't been dating much since. Penny, who worked with Julie on her income tax preparations, generally got together with Julie during Super Bowl weekend each January and combined taxes with the football party. At the party, Julie was pursued by a tall, dark-haired, witty charmer who didn't want to take "no" for an answer. She managed to keep him at bay until the following May when she finally agreed to have lunch with him.

It was a romantic whirlwind for a while and Julie's vulnerable side gave in to the attention, the promises, the fun, and the hopes new love delivers. He knew the right things to say, the best things to do. He was fun to be with and he eventually won her heart. Shakespeare wrote, "Look with thine ears," but, such advice is useless in the throes of sexual attraction and new love. Furthest from her mind were the depths to which a con artist would stoop.

In addition to performing, as she had done before, in the air show at the Hamilton Wings of Victory in 1989, Julie rented the use of Otis Spunkmeyer's DC-3 and made plans for a magical wedding in the clouds. As a performer, she was the center of attention, encircled by persons who truly appreciated and admired her. As a woman, she relished the relationship and chose this particular idyllic spot on the northwest corner of San Francisco Bay for its beauty, for the romance of flying over the Golden Gate and the Bay, and for a memorable wedding performed at altitude surrounded with Julie's closest friends. Infatuated, it didn't occur to her she was marrying a cheat, a liar, and a thief.

Judith Lund, her excellent attorney and fellow pilot, said, "The man was bad; he was nothing but a crook. Oh, he was a charmer; but, he was a crook!"

Within six months of their marriage, Julie knew she had made a mistake. Her husband wasn't working, but he had her believing he was. He pretended to be an insurance salesman, dressing appropriately and leaving the house each morning. He wasn't bringing in a penny toward living expenses and he was continually asking her to "loan" him money he somehow failed to repay.

Although she never saw him do it, others told her they'd seen him use drugs and Julie certainly lived with a person who was volatile; he could be laughing one moment and crying the next. She saw him taking pills, but he called them blood pressure pills.

They had discussed whether he had been married and, later, she recognized the innocence with which she had accepted his protestations of love and his assurance he'd *been* married and had gone through a divorce. She failed to demand to see divorce papers.

When Northwest Airlines asked whether the children entered on her health insurance were living under her roof, she was flabbergasted. She hadn't known there *were* children; she'd never seen them and, no, to her knowledge they didn't live anywhere nearby. Her name was forged on the application for coverage.

But, the scenario grew even more serious and more threatening. She went for a photo shoot over Lake Tahoe and one of the smoke grenades on her T-34's wing, instead of emitting a long plume of billowing smoke, burst into flames. Fortunately, it burned and dropped *off* of the wing, but not before having threatened the entire flight and Julie's life. How could black match, a fuse, have gotten into her wingtip?

Her mechanic, Neil Weaver, had given her husband a part-time job in his shop. When Neil found a can of lubricating oil jammed into the tail section of her T-34, he and Julie both new the dangers of having a "foreign object" rolling near the bell crank for her aircraft elevator. Her aircraft controls could have been jammed. The oil had been purchased from a hardware chain with no stores in California.

In typical entrepreneurial fervor, Julie had looked about for an investment and had settled on the small "Free Spirit Yogurt Shop" near Cameron Park Airport. Associated with a delicatessen owned by her friends, Harry and Kate Allen, her "Free Spirit Yogurt Shop" was kept open six days a week. She held it for eighteen months. The Allens told Julie about her husband staggering into their deli one night and bragging about plans to steal her Beech Bonanza Debonair, her company support aircraft. He also let slip intentions to serve her with divorce papers, saying, "he was going to clean her out" and "she wouldn't know what hit her."

Finally, the owner of a local restaurant confided he was taking some of the waitresses home with him when Julie was out of town. Reportedly, the women said he would show them Julie's picture and say, "This was my wife. She was killed in a plane crash."

"He was planning this all along," Julie said, "and he had it very well engineered. Thank goodness, with God's help, I got the insight from close friends and acquaintances and brought it all crashing down around his shoulders."

Divorce papers –drawn up as early as November 1991 – were served to Julie in March of 1992. As the papers were being served, Julie got a call from Neil Weaver. "Your husband is here demanding the keys to your Debonair."

"Don't give them to him!" she insisted.

It is not difficult to imagine the anguish Julie felt with each new revelation. She must have grown exasperated with herself for having been duped. When people asked her how such an intelligent person could be so fooled, she said, "Don't even go there. When you fall for someone, marry, and place your trust, you just can't believe the lies until finally things loom so large they cannot be ignored. I discovered the tip of the iceberg within six months. It took longer to get to the whole truth."

Prenuptial Agreement

Luckily, Julie had insisted on securing a prenuptial agreement (PNA) before she was married at the Hamilton Air Force Base Wings of Victory Air Show in 1989. Believing in her husband-to-be, she had flown off radiantly and willingly in Otis Spunkmeyer's classic airplane, her wedding gown beautifully cut, the tulle of a veil hanging gently over her back and shoulders.

The PNA, signed by both of them, was nine pages long and detailed everything Julie owned prior to the wedding and would remain hers – especially the company she built from scratch. It listed numerous assets.

When the property settlement trial finally called her before a judge, Julie brought nine witnesses and a lawyer to the courtroom. Her husband showed up with his mother. As the plaintiff, he had the first opportunity to address the court. He tried to pass himself off as the program manager for Julie's air show business. He said, "I made her what she is."

Julie snapped, "I had my air show and Mopar sponsorship before I ever *met* him."

Her lawyer quieted her. "You'll get your chance. Stay calm."

He brought letters addressed to various air show management venues. Julie had never seen the letters before and had not authorized them. Tellingly, she could prove he had never been on the payroll.

"He could have typed those letters in a hotel room the night before," she said. "He was building a case, scheming right under my nose. I'd no idea he was going after my business. I made a huge mistake giving him check-writing privileges on my business checks. Fortunately, we never had a joint personal account.

"At the time, I received approximately $140,000 in sponsorship monies and it generally came in two installments. We discovered he was holding the last check, undoubtedly waiting for $70,000 to be deposited.

"When he took the stand, he said he was *forced* to sign papers, knew nothing of any PNA, and had been told they were corporation papers, which were drawn up in the same year.

"My crew chief, Larry Littlepage wrote an explanatory note describing the start of my business in 1980. His letter contradicted the crook's false statements completely. My current crew, Ron and Judy McLane, were there to defend me, too. For protection and support, they even moved into my air show trailer in my back yard for months prior to the trial.

"My former attorney's secretary testified in my behalf. She said my husband knew full well about the PNA and had even helped her write it. She told he knew exactly what he was signing and was signing in person when she was notarizing the document. The original was in her boss' office safe.

"I'd never faced anything like this. Judy Lund had loaned me a videotape of demonstrated depositions so that I would be somewhat prepared. She helped a great deal with this grueling, wretched episode in my life. I was remonstrated, 'Don't embellish things. Don't get emotional. Just answer the questions you are asked.'"

"The judge was a no-nonsense man. As the trial began, he wanted to know how I'd gotten started, wanted to see pictures of the airplane, and asked what air show piloting was all about.

"At one point I said, 'I've never had anything given to me. I've earned everything; I restored this airplane myself, I started my business myself; I was orphaned at the age of 15, my dad...' and I started crying.

"He said, 'We'll take a recess.'"

I said, 'No, your honor. I'll pull it together.' I finally did.

"At a later recess Judy Lund said, 'You cried just enough.'

"But, it was from my heart. This man was trying to ruin me and we'd been married two years. Two *years*!"

"It was awful! I was granted a Dissolution of Marriage at the end of 1992. Harriet Fox, my tax consultant, warned me they would garnish my wages to pay for his arrears in child support and his debts if I didn't get a certificate of dissolution. One day she saw me when I was looking particularly beat. She said, 'You let this get to your health and then you will have lost everything. Please eat. You have to get your act together.'

"So, I had to defend and fight for all the things already rightfully mine. And I had to take care of my health at the same time. All I could think was he could have been typing those letters for the last year and a half, always building himself a case. I discovered he was going after half of my company. He asked for spousal support of $4,500 per month. The guy was out of his mind! Half of my retirement for a fraud of a two-year marriage? It is so very scary when everything of importance in your life, including savings set aside for retirement, risks being taken away.

"Once we had the dissolution we faced two more years until a settlement trial could occur. When the trial was over and the jerk lost, big time, he declared bank-ruptcy and ended up stiffing his attorney for $55,000. By the time it was all over, I had to pay $64,000 in lawyer fees. I called Gladys Hood, my 'Minnesota Mom,' and yelled, 'I'm *free!*'

"The judge was there specifically to address the question of dissolution, but before we left he suggested I use my time and money to get the guy thrown in jail. He was guilty of forgery, fraud, and bigamy, but I never followed up. I just hope our paths never cross again in this world. I was so glad to be free I could hardly stand it. How could I have been so blind?"

CHAPTER FOURTEEN: CLIPPED WINGS SOAR

After having built her successful business and having been thrust into prominence as an outstanding air show performer, was it fair that Julie's American Aerobatics, Incorporated faced extinction because of situations entirely out of her control? After having clutched tenaciously to keep it from being wrested out of her hands in the messy marriage annulment, did she deserve once again to face failure when, in April 1999, a Sky Warriors' Air Combat Maneuvers (ACM) Beech T-34 crashed in Rydal, Georgia?

Although fatal crashes make headlines across the country, reverberations from the April fatalities affected every T-34 owner in the United States. No one was spared from the maelstrom.

Black Summer of 1999

The National Transportation Safety Board reported the fatal crash was "preceded by an in-flight separation of the right wing." In-flight separation strikes terror into pilots. Taught to recover from unusual attitudes, to glide in the event of an engine failure, and to make an off-airport landing in case of the failure of retractable gear, most pilots expect the unexpected. Most fly with alternatives in mind and remain flexible and prepared for emergencies. But, when a wing separates from the fuselage of an airplane, the pilot is left to scramble for an exit, assuming one can be reached in the wild gyrations that ensue, and take to a parachute, assuming there is one aboard and strapped at the ready. Bailout is dubious, of course, as a fuselage with only one wing enters a rotational mode; a safe exit from the spinning craft would be nothing short of miraculous.

What caused the wing to separate? How was the aircraft being flown? In what situation was a structural failure of the normally sturdy training aircraft induced?

Those probing questions were raised, but first, in a knee-jerk reaction to prevent any other T-34 aircraft from structural failure and to keep other pilots from being fatally injured, the Federal Aviation Administration issued an Airworthiness Directive (an AD) placing airspeed and G-load limitations on all T-34s and called for *no* aerobatics. Raytheon issued a "mandatory" bulletin for all T-34 owners and required the inspection of critical fatigue locations on T-34 aircraft.

Examination of the Rydal wing spar showed multiple incidences of fatigue and, on 5 May 2000 – thirteen *months* after the accident – the FAA published a proposed AD "mandating Raytheon's recommended wing spar inspections." It was 30 July of 2002 before the FAA issued a "Special Airworthiness Information Bulletin" listing approved Alternative Methods of Compliance (AMOCs) and extended the AD compliance deadline. Like a case in a court of law, the wheels of accident investigation rolled slowly. From May to September 1999, however, Julie Clark's American Aerobatics, Incorporated was threatened and Julie suffered excruciating loss.

General Aviation Modifications, Incorporated, offered this brief background on 18 August 1999: "In the past few months, Raytheon, the FAA, the NTSB, and others have participated in the investigation of the causes surrounding the April 1999 Sky Warrior's accident involving the loss of two individuals when the right wing failed. Mr. Charlie Nogle, President of the T-34 Association and other Nogle

184

family members have diligently participated in these efforts, giving of their expertise and reporting numerous findings, recommendations and intentions of the investigation back to the T-34 Association. We are extremely grateful and fortunate to have their support."

Julie echoes those sentiments. She couldn't have managed without the help of the Nogles. Among their other generosities, it was Charlie and Jud Nogle who delivered her wings to be examined, replaced them on the T-34, and then had to remove them and deliver them to the FAA once again when a repeat examination was requested. En route back to Illinois with the wings loaded on a flatbed trailer, Charlie, who was towing the trailer, had the disquieting experience of watching his son Jud lose control of his vehicle on rain-swept streets and slide into a ditch. Fortunately, neither Jud nor the wings were injured in the accident.

Of vital importance to Julie, the AD restricted T-34s to loadings from zero to 2.5 positive Gs, to normal category operations, and it specifically restricted T-34s from being flown in aerobatics. In speed restrictions, it limited the never-exceed speed to 152 knots and required special placards and airspeed indicator markings. This wiped clean her slate of the performances she had scheduled, immediately affected her annual income, added expensive compliance maintenance repairs to her costs, and threatened her long-term relationship with and funding by her sponsors. Without putting her sponsors' logos and products before the public, she was of little value to those who invested their money in her. It was a frightening prospect.

The FAA and the NTSB continued to investigate the accident. Finding stress in both wings of the accident craft, investigators agreed the recent stress of simulated air combat was at fault, not the age of the aircraft.

"I came so close to losing my entire business," Julie admitted. "American Aerobatics means the world to me. The thought of closing my hangar doors just about wiped me out.

"We were grounded on 28 May 1999 and the tension was awful. Of *course* I regretted two men had lost their lives. Every pilot would like to see zero accidents

185

in aviation's safety column. However, being grounded spelled another horrific period in my life. I flew my T-28 to the FAA Certification Office in Wichita, Kansas, and urged representatives to recognize restrictions cannot be mandated without reference to inspection criteria to allow the problem to be addressed. Knowing my T-34 was flown more regularly and probably as vigorously as anyone's, the FAA requested my airplane for inspection for that purpose.

"They conducted exploratory examinations and I took my T-34 to Nogle and Black Aviation in Tuscola, Illinois for wing removal and delivery to Wichita, Kansas, for further study. There they drilled into the spars and evaluated the likelihood of having to maintain the limitations imposed. I fervently prayed they wouldn't find stress fractures like those found in the wing spars of the Sky Warriors' T-34s *and* they wouldn't cause damage in the drilling process. I spent hours traveling to Washington, DC, to Wichita, Kansas, and to Nogle and Black Aviation. Charlie and Jud Nogle were hugely helpful to me.

"My airplane was being investigated under microscopes – eddy current testing, stress testing, examining minute inspections for fractures and cracks. I knew my T-34 wouldn't be released for several months, despite the publishing of a Service Bulletin. They were looking for something that wasn't there.

"In letting them investigate my airplane copiously, I felt like a mother hen. I'd owned my airplane for 24 years. It had flown in air shows for 20 years. Mine were the original spars and had 11,000 hours. If anyone's wing spar was well used and liable to display fatigue, it was mine. I dreaded what they might find. *They're going to find cracked wings. They're going to find bad spars. Oh, my airplane's going to be grounded forever. It's going to end up as a weather vane on top of my house, displayed like surplus airplanes are mounted at U.S. Air Force Bases.*

"On the other hand, I purchased it right from the U.S. Government. The T-34 has a sturdy, well-built airframe and this particular T-34 has been well cared for. I had to be patient. I knew if *mine* came out clean, the average T-34 was going to be fine unless something had occurred during its military years and caused it to be overstressed, over-G'd, or overloaded. Metal has memory and it *will* fatigue.

"A song came out in 1999 and every time I heard it, I cried. One of the verses was, 'So take these broken wings and let me fly again.' It's a positive song and I still hear it once in a while, but it tore me up. I was *grounded*..."

All of the major aviation organizations became involved. In part, the Aircraft Owners and Pilots Association (AOPA) issued an estimate of the expenses in time and the financial ramifications of the AD, explaining:

"The proposed AD mandates initial and repetitive inspections and immediate replacement of cracked or damaged wing spars. The FAA estimates that compliance with the initial inspection will require 241 hours, while compliance with the repetitive inspection (recurring every 80 hours time in service) will take an additional 31 hours. At the FAA's standard estimate of $60/hr. for labor, cost of compliance with the provisions of Raytheon's Service Bulletin is $14,460 per airplane for the initial inspection and $1,860/airplane every 80 hours Time In Service thereafter. If the inspections reveal cracks, the wing spar must be replaced. The FAA estimates that each replacement will cost over $14,000." To date, replacement through one of the four AMOCs is estimated to cost approximately $26,000.

The Bloody Accident

Some facts stated at the time of the Sky Warriors' T-34 crash were irrefutable:

> Metal fatigue of key wing components near the root caused wing failure.
> The airplane involved had 8,200 hours of total flying time.
> No special requirements for airplanes used in simulated air combat existed.
> The T-34 went into service with the U.S. Air Force in 1954 or 1955.
> The T-34 flew approximately 4,000 flight hours as a primary trainer.
> The T-34 was in private hands for 20 years prior to purchase in 1990 for use in simulated air combat.

The T-34 flew approximately 4,000 hours in simulated "dogfights."

Some questions were more speculative and difficult to answer. A popular amusement for pilots and non-flyers alike has been to strap on a sleek, racy-looking aircraft and engage in mock air combat. The Rydal, Georgia T-34 had two men aboard; it was flying for the express purpose of simulating combat and attempting to use electronic means to defeat or "shoot down" opponents in other T-34s who were attempting to be victorious as well. Were the combatants pulling more G-forces than the aircraft was meant to sustain? Over time, had other combatants over-stressed these same aircraft?

One customer who had enjoyed simulated aerial combat prior to the fatal accident at Sky Warriors in Georgia posted a photo essay on the Internet. He wrote about "aerial laser combat," likening it to laser tag, using a laser beam as a "weapon" to "simulate a battle." He added the "same concept and technology was installed in fighter aircraft." Acknowledging that no flying experience was necessary, he went on to admit that, in his words, a client would "perform basic dog-fighting techniques taught" prior to take off. He finished with, "This is Top Gun for non-pilots and…one HELL of a ride."

Fighter **Aircraft**

Although it was implied glowingly that the "Yeehaah bad-boy" was like "WWII Fighter Aircraft.," the T-34 is a *trainer* and a significant difference in design exists between trainers and fighters. Should a training airplane be used by any commercial endeavor to simulate what it was not designed to do?

On the world wide web, Texas Air Aces, a company focused upon air safety, advertises, "…Then it's out to the flight line for a close-up look at your T-34 fighter," adding, "…one of the hottest fighter trainer aircraft ever built." Much value is received by flight students who take advanced courses in aviation safety and unusual attitude recovery. Must it include "fighter combat simulation" in a 1950s trainer?

Terry Brennan, editor of *The Mentor Monitor* and currently on the Board of

Directors of the T-34 Association, attended a briefing at Sky Warriors, at which the briefer said, "The first rule, other than the fact that the power shall not exceed 25-inches of manifold pressure, is that there are no rules."

Obviously, as Julie demonstrates in her every air show, the T-34 can be flown in aerobatic maneuvers. She said, 'This is an aerobatic airplane, built for the military and built like a stout brick outhouse." It is indeed capable of smooth, properly flown aerobatics. Pilots must be trained to maneuver through the three axes and the four forces of flight. It does *not* have an inverted fuel system, so the T-34 cannot sustain inverted flight, nor does Julie whip it into a frenzied, frantic series of maneuvers designed to overstress the aircraft, overstress the pilot, and shorten the likelihood that the two could continue to thrill air show audiences all over North America.

"In 1985," she recalled, "after my performance at EAA's Convention in Oshkosh, Charlie Nogle urged me to stop snap-rolling my airplane at the top of my 'heart in the sky,' reminding me that these T-34s are aging aircraft. From that time on my heart created of smoke has been made up of a loop with a slow roll at the top. This makes the heart less crisp, but makes for safer aerobatics. I haven't snapped 'Wally' since."

There have been several entrepreneurs who have promoted the T-34 in simulated combat experiences with capable and knowledgeable pilots at the controls. Perhaps there are better platforms to use for this "Top Gun" stab at thrills for would-be fighter jocks.

The bleak year of 1999 dragged on. Non-destructive testing was required every 80 hours. Although the AD was reported, it took months for it to actually see the light of publication and when it hit the streets it contained 63 *pages* of requirements with which an aircraft owner was required to comply. The T-34 fleet hung in limbo while Julie's aircraft underwent scrutiny and was found to be clean. She came within hours of never flying air shows again because it was affecting her airplane so gravely.

Her secretary C.J. Freeland recommended they take the crew trailer to each of their scheduled shows. There Julie could sign autographs, promote her sponsors, put the MOPAR name in front of the audiences as she'd contracted to do, and demonstrate her eagerness to be *there*, even without her airplane. Josh Blay and Lindsey Koron, her ground crew, went with her as she put in her appearances. At EAA AirVenture in 1999, the T-34 Association had planned on celebrating the 50th anniversary of the T-34 by staging a massive fly-over. Julie was depressed to have her T-34 in pieces, but was gratified for more than four T-34 owners who offered to let her fly their Mentors in the gaggle of 60 airplanes filling the sky over Oshkosh, Wisconsin. Happy for the chance, she took to the sky like a wild duck joining a flock.

Desperation

Finally, Julie went directly to Jane Garvey, the Administrator of the Federal Aviation Administration. To office subordinates' questions: "Did you send a fax? Did you have an appointment?" she said, "No! I came here to talk with her and I want to talk with her right now."

She continued, "To the Administrator, I said, 'You people are taking away my livelihood and I've done everything to comply. I've spent $40,000 of my own money. I've been to Raytheon several times. We have *torn* my airplane apart – the wings have been taken off and completely opened up. Nothing like that has been done since they *built* the airplane. They saw the interior created in this airplane in 1956. It's clean! It has been given a good bill of health and, now that we know what is under the skin of that airplane, the FAA is not going to let me go fly it in the way that it was designed to fly! To have Raytheon clear my airplane and to have the FAA say that I am still to be restricted to 'No Aerobatics, two-and-a-half Gs,' is ridiculous!'

"I paid for *all* of the labor that was done. I can show a myriad of pictures of this airplane opened up for the entire world to see."

"'I donated *my* wings for this testing and can produce all the photos of having drilled out the spars. This is an invasive procedure. If the drilling is not done correctly, the spars can be ruined. If the spars go, the airplane is *history*. You can't find T-34 spars for a 50-year-old airplane lying on a shelf somewhere."

She had a head of steam going. Having dealt with a myriad of representatives, she took her complaints to the top. [Three years later, at the annual convention of Women In Aviation, International, she sought out Jane Garvey once again. She said, "I'd like to get in her face again with a "Thank You" instead of getting in her face with a complaint.]

Julie was anguished. She was grounded for four and a half months and had been told that, were she to miss flying her air show performance at the very special Mopar 17th Annual Dodge Vintage Festival in Limerock Park, Connecticut over Labor Day Weekend her sponsorship would have to be reevaluated. She said, "I interpreted the warning to mean my sponsorship was in jeopardy. I have cherished their sponsorship for 13 *years*. It is my *livelihood!* They were going to make me the Poster Child for the Emergency AD like they made Bob Hoover the Poster Child for FAA Physicals. Most frustratingly, the restrictions were going to erase my business and had *nothing to do with me*!

Yet, the fall-out from the Sky Warriors' fatalities resulted in Julie's cancellation of performances at 14 air shows. She said, "At an average of from $8,000 to $10,000 per show, those cancellations represented a financial loss of between $115,000 and $140,000."

As in any small business, Josh, Lindsey, and C.J. had to be maintained on the payroll. Fixed costs don't disappear when the revenue takes a dive. She admit-

Julie with "Ernie" and "Mollie"

ted, "If the Nogles hadn't helped me so generously, I couldn't have waged the effort I did. If Mopar hadn't given me my sponsorship money at the beginning of the year, which I always get in a lump sum in March or April, I never could have afforded $40,000 of my own money to pay for the research and to use my airplane as the guinea pig."

EAA Warbirds Of America

Offering a great deal of support was the Experimental Aircraft Association and its Warbirds of America. The Warbirds began as a club uniting owners of WWII fighter aircraft and has mushroomed into an organization that welcomes owners of every variety of military craft. At the height of the Emergency AD controversy, EAA's Warbirds of America printed the following:

"Yet another area of government activity in which our organization has been actively involved is the issue of the T-34 spar AD. Members of our division, together with EAA staff, have met with the FAA and Raytheon, both at Oshkosh and Oklahoma City, to determine a suitable solution to the issue of spar cracks. We also have designated funds to pay for an independent metallurgist to study the problem and help with a solution at a reasonable cost.

"Metal fatigue in aging aircraft is a problem that is not going to go away and will clearly become more of a problem in the future for all of us who operate ex-military aircraft. This, and other important topics, will be on the agenda at the National Warbird Operators Conference slated for 1-4 March 2001 in Washington, DC. The Warbirds of America has been the prime mover in the organization and operation of this meeting. We opted to hold it in Washington so FAA personnel could attend without the constraints of travel budgets. A number of key FAA officials responsible for regulation and operation of warbird aircraft have committed to attend this annual gathering. A number of government metallurgy experts are expected to attend this meeting, as are experts from the private sector. ... It promises to be an exciting and enlightening program.

"...The approach that EAA Warbirds has taken with the FAA has been not one of confrontation, but rather consultation. Our goal is to establish ourselves as a resource for them and, at the same time, to do everything we can to prevent any further encroachment on our privilege to fly warbird aircraft. Unfortunately, numbers count in Washington. That is why our relationship with EAA is crucial to maintaining our flying privileges. Having 170,000-plus active members in a large, respected organization such as EAA gives us the attention that we could never achieve as a small group. Our work in these areas benefits not only our membership, but the rest of the warbird community as well. ..."

With apologies to Ayn Rand, "Atlas *Shrugged!*"

When Julie discovered the restrictions had been lifted , on 3 September 1999, she burst into tears again. As soon as possible, she climbed into "Wally" and flew like her heart was going to break. She said, "I took off and practiced my act, crying like a baby. It was unreal. Some of the top aerobatic stars understood what I had been going through – Bob Hoover, Wayne Handley...

"Wayne asked, 'Are you okay?'

"I told him, 'Not really. I'm doing the best that I can.'

"He said, 'I keep reading about what is happening to you and you aren't even the reason that all of this has come down!'"

A Postscript

Unfortunately, the convoluted and threatening processes weren't over. On 19 November 2003, another fatal crash and reported in-flight break-up of another Beech T-34 drew all eyes to Conroe, Texas. The Mentor had been one of two aircraft from Texas Air Aces and was piloted by former U.S.A.F. combat pilot Don Wylie, the founder in 1995 of Aviation Safety Training, which was designed to assist experienced pilots to handle unexpected and dangerous flight occurrences.

With his client and passenger, Airborne Express pilot William Eisenhauer of Centerville, Ohio, Wylie crashed after the T-34 lost its right wing during "upset recovery training." According to the website for Texas Air Aces, flights in T-34 aircraft offered safety and formation flight training, but the home page stated, "No flight experience required. You're right in the middle of a head-to-head air combat. It'll be the fight of your life!" and continued to invite customers to meet a "veteran military pilot" who would be "your ACI, Air Combat Instructor."

This second tragedy resonated throughout the T-34 Association rapidly. As the investigation by the National Transportation Safety Board is still underway at this writing, future actions remain to be seen.

A representative of the T-34 Association, Incorporated, wrote to the FAA's Wichita Aircraft Certification Office. The letter stated, in part, "The only T-34 aircraft to exhibit any form of main or rear spar fatigue or failure have been aircraft used in commercial simulated air combat or 'Upset training.' ...It is not necessary that the majority of the T-34 fleet suffer further restrictions. Numerous witnesses and paying customers have reported that both aircraft involved in the fatal accidents were repeatedly flown outside the certificated envelope.

"...At least a half-dozen, non-air combat T-34 aircraft have been inspected in accordance with the *full* Raytheon Aircraft Service Bulletin, and none has been found to have fatigue. One of these aircraft, N134JC, has been flown for nearly 12,000 hours, much of which includes air show aerobatics. [This is a direct reference to Julie's aircraft.]

"...The T-34 Association, Inc, thanks the FAA for giving us the opportunity to respond to the 'Airworthiness Concern Sheet' and, if in the end the FAA feels that it is appropriate and necessary to impart further restrictions, we would suggest that this could be done by the FAA requiring the AMOC holders to issue 'Temporary Instructions for Continued Airworthiness,' re-imposing the restrictions of AD 99-12-02 and AD 2001-13-18 until a revised AMOC is issued and completed."

Mayday!

Although it consumed her emotionally, Julie wasn't free to spend all of her time working the T-34 AD problem. She continued with her airline career and she also had her T-28 Trojan. But, as if the dark clouds hanging over the T-34 fiasco were permanent fixtures, she had an incident in her T-28 in the same summer.

Unbelievably, in July 1999 and en route to the EAA AirVenture, Julie's T-28 blew its engine. Josh Blay was a passenger in her back seat. Headed away from Kenosha, Wisconsin, Julie and other T-28 pilots had joined on one another. "We were flying in a 9-ship formation and concentrating as usual. I was not aware of a professional photographer in the back seat of the lead, whose wing I was flying. Later I had a chance to see pictures of the entire episode.

"We were about 90 miles away from Oshkosh when I had an emergency in my T-28. I knew it was bad. Smoke pouring from a round engine is very bad. The chip light came on and I started losing power. I radioed 'Mayday' and immediately pulled up and out of the formation. The cardinal rule when dealing with an engine failure is to climb, climb, *climb!* I said to Josh over the intercom, 'Josh, right now bailing out is *not* an option!'

"I'd lost all my oil. My engine had failed. I asked lead, 'Where the hell are we?'

"He said, 'Turn left to a heading of 220 degrees, Julie. You're eleven miles from Kenosha.'

"I said, 'Eleven miles? I'll never make it.'

"I contacted the Kenosha, Wisconsin, Tower at 119.4 and said, 'I'm eleven miles to the northeast. I've had an engine failure. I don't know if I'm going to make it to Kenosha or not.'

"The controller responded and asked, 'Say number of souls on board, amount of fuel, and your N number.'

I told her, 'I'm a big yellow airplane. Just look for me!'

"I had my hands full. It was nerve-wracking. Luckily, my prop never quit turning, but I had absolutely zero power. If your prop stops, you have a monstrous speed brake out front. They say, 'Throw a brick out of a T-28 and the brick will follow *you* down.'

"Fortunately, we made it to Kenosha.Once we got onto the ground the airplane was streaked with oil all the way out to the tailhook. I was very fortunate that my mechanic from California, Bob Grant, happened to be at the convention. He came down from Oshkosh, pulled off the prop, which was filled with metal. The number 3 piston had blown a hole right through the cylinder. The engine was trashed!

"Kenosha and the Jet Center at Kenosha, owned by Ken Ross, was home to the airplane for five months. Ken had owned a T-34 and a T-28 and proved to be a good friend. He kindly didn't charge me hangar rent for the entire time, but the repair bill came to over $52,000. The summer of 1999 dealt me a horrendous financial loss. To have an engine failure on the T-28 after all the T-34 fleet had been through was just *way* too much.

"Later, the photographer was asked whether he'd noticed the smoke from my failed engine. He said, 'I just figured she was blowing show smoke.'

"I don't *have* show smoke in my T-28!"

Not the First Accident Waiting to Happen

In her earlier flights out of Western Sierra in Fresno, Julie recalled ferrying a Cessna 210 from the factory in Wichita, Kansas, back to Fresno. She said, "I felt responsible to check out the new craft and to make certain that everything worked properly.

"I opted to climb to 17,500 feet, just below 18,000 (Flight Level 180) in order to avoid having to file IFR (Instrument Flight Rules). I wanted to check out the oxygen system and get acquainted with the aircraft. I donned the oxygen mask and had my seat kicked back. I was thumbing through the Operator's Manual. All of a sudden, the airplane pitched violently. Instantly, I regretted I'd pushed the seat back. I whipped off the oxygen mask and leaned forward... fast!

"'What in hell's going on here?' I tried to disconnect the autopilot and it wouldn't disconnect. The trim wheel was whirring and I reached to try to stop it with my hand. We were diving like crazy. I kept pulling back on the yoke, but I knew I might overstress and pull its wings off. I was fighting it like mad and I finally turned off the master switch.

"I hadn't been talking to anybody. I was somewhere over New Mexico, descending rapidly. I was freaking out because the airspeed was really climbing out of sight. I was trying to pull back incrementally: pull, release it; pull back, release it. I'd shut everything off, but the trim wheel motor was still buzzing. Why? There was no power to the master. The airspeed indicator went on around the dial and started around the second time. The needle circled past zero and reached all the way to 110 mph for the *second* go-around. I thought, 'Oh, my God, I'm dead!'

"*Finally*, I was able to get it under control and the trim wheel stopped turning. Then smoke started oozing out from under the panel. Something had really self-destructed! I pressed on toward home and, when things had settled down a bit, I looked behind at the tail to make sure it was okay. The fairing on the ventral fin looked bent.

"I didn't want to talk to anybody. I continued to Fresno and landed. Then I

197

had to admit that something awful had happened. It turned out to be an autopilot failure. Thank God I was high! But the stupidity on my part was to have had that seat pushed back. I never did that again!

"The manager asked, 'Why didn't you shut off the autopilot?' Duh. That's the first thing I did. 'Why didn't you turn off the radio?' I turned off the radio master. I turned off the battery switch. I did everything but shut off the fuel. I told him, 'I don't know why the autopilot motor was still running. With all the gyrations that I went through, I think the ventral fin was damaged.'

"When he asked, 'How high did your airspeed go?' I said, 'I don't want to tell you.'

"'Julie. How *fast?*'

"'It circled the gauge completely and reached 110 a second time.'

"I thought I was done! Finally, the mechanic came out. He was holding a circuit board and he said, 'This is the main power supply to the autopilot, all the radios. Look at it.'

"It was burned to a crisp. I hadn't wanted to confess, but I knew I had to be truthful so that they could check the structural integrity of the aircraft. They did completely remove the wing fairings and they checked everything. But, I was most fortunate to coax the yoke. I'd pull, then release, reenter the dive; pull back, release, start diving again. I knew enough to be gradual about it.

"It seems women pilots will never avoid being questioned

Sought after as a speaker, Julie addresses an Education Session at an annual convention of Women in Aviation, International

about mechanical knowledge. Even if we possess A&P mechanic certificates, we'll always be questioned in our analysis and judgment. Men have physical abilities women don't have; they possess strength. We women are smaller and lacking in physical prowess, perhaps; but we're just as strong in brain power."

11 September 2001

The tragedies and losses of lives on 11 September brought more than incomprehension and fury from Julie. Her gut reactions were visceral. Her own father's murder was replayed again in her mind and the thought of entering her own airline cockpit after such traumatic events was more than she could bear. Rick Toscano, the Chief Pilot in Minneapolis, gave her a leave of absence. He knew about her father and knew how difficult it would be for her to try to come to grips with the insanity of terrorists who, in the name of their god, could enter an airline cockpit and overcome, batter, and perhaps slit the throats of innocent pilots. Such acts went far beyond any rational concept of civilized mankind and displayed hatred far deeper than any she'd ever thought possible. She grieved deeply and lamented, too, that in the raising of firefighters and police officers to superhero status, virtually no attention was paid to the pilots who underwent horrific deaths and might have fought valiantly for the lives of the passengers with whom they'd been entrusted.

She grieved for the lives lost; she grieved, anew, for the mother and the father she'd lost. Did she want to carry a gun? No, she'd never handled a gun; she didn't want to think of having to use it in the cockpit that had been the scene of so much of her pleasure, so much of her capability. Thirty-five years of her life had been devoted as a professional in aviation. She'd been trained to deal with anyone who might have pushed into the cockpit to divert her craft to, say, Cuba. But, nothing had prepared the pilots who met their doom on 11 September. Just as her father had been the first to be shot at the controls and to have his entire crew and passengers die, this was another first with which to deal. It was unthinkable!

Terrorists! Assassins! How could anyone prepare to face insanity in the confines of a cockpit? To come to grips with any so consumed with hatred as to intentionally destroy pilots, crewmembers, the airplane, the passengers, humans on the ground, and the sites that represented the nation of which she was so proud was beyond comprehension. The horror, relived, brought back all of the anguish of her youth.

Time had to be taken. Time, once again, had to be depended upon to heal. Luckily, she also had her deep Christian convictions.

The Show Will Go On

On 9 October 2003, Julie stepped aboard the Airbus A 320 to fly from Sacramento to Minneapolis in what had been designated as her final flight as Captain for Northwest Airlines. At the time of her retirement, she held Seniority #277 out of 5,500 Northwest pilots, not counting the more than 900 who had been furloughed and were still awaiting recall at the end of 2003. She could be proud of her achievements and of a career well done.

She would savor the joy of her final flight for a long time to come. Flying with her were nine of her closest friends and family members. She was especially joyous to have both of her sisters, Judy Grilli and Sharon De Vos, her "Minnesota Mom" Gladys Hood, and, the man in her life, her best friend, Allan Thomas. Allan, who has shared many a great experience with her, also shares her love of aviation. Having flown as a Marine Corps helicopter pilot in Vietnam, Allan was a US Air Force Reserve pilot and logistics officer who had retired in the rank of Colonel in 1998. When he flew with Julie in the T-28, he asked, "Do you provide crying towels?"

Julie wanted to know why and Allan responded, "You are taking me back 35 years to the last time I flew a T-28 during my military pilot training."

Having delighted in the celebration of her retirement at the party on 15 October 2003 – this time surrounded by hundreds of friends and associates – Julie couldn't help but be linked forever with the fact that she celebrated the culmination of her airline career during the auspicious Centennial of Powered Flight. She entertained her guests a mere two months short of the 17 December Wright Brothers' 100th Anniversary of their celebrated first flight in a heavier-than-air powered craft. Having only lived for half of their celebrated century, Julie could be justifiably proud of having contributed so greatly to the remarkable history of aviation. Although women were involved in aviation from the start of powered flight – the Wright Brothers themselves were aided by the encouragement of their sister, Katharine – women weren't given the chance to serve as U.S. airline pilots until 1973 and Julie was at the cutting edge of that achievement.

She could look back, marveling at the airways she'd flown, the airplanes she'd conquered, the family members she'd cherished, and the friends and acquaintances she'd gained. She could also look forward, knowing that shutting the door to her airline career meant opening wider the opportunities to continue to excite air show fans with her aerial performances.

Julie admitted, "You know? I've never grown tired of flying. Even when I was fortunate enough to be flying jet airliners, I enjoyed flying small airplanes and loved the feeling of joy that I felt to be airborne and to be free. Air is a fabulous element. I cherish every moment that I've been able to wrap it around my airplane and to thrust my airplane into its magical qualities.

"I think that airline pilots who spend all spare time with their investments or golf games are simply bus drivers. I have more admiration for the airline types who build and fly their own experimental kit- or plans-built aircraft, the ones who do competition aerobatics or who restore antique or classic birds. These are pilots in the true sense of the word. These are pilots who really love flying.

"Until I transitioned to the Airbus, I

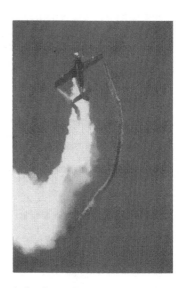

Julie, from _World Airshow News_

hand flew my DC-9 up to altitude or at least to 18,000 feet, Flight Level 180, before clicking on the autopilot. I waited to the last moment to use the Flight Mode Annunciator (FMA) and to let the airplane's technology take over to level off, turn, do the departure, and follow the speed restrictions if there were some. Too many pilots flip on that autopilot before reaching 3,000 feet and they don't click it off until the last thing before they are ready to land. I'm just not that kind of pilot. I truly enjoy *flying*."

To Inspire Even One

Julie Clark has watched the sparkle of admiration shine from the eyes of the young who have clustered around her at the end of each of her performances. She said, "Even though I haven't had any kids of my own, children seem to gravitate to me readily. I've been called 'The Pied Piper' at air shows because, after I fly, kids will follow me to the air show trailer and I'll sign autographs until the last little kid goes home. I've even had one little guy stop me when I was taxiing out to depart from Oshkosh. I saw the child wave to me, wanting me to stop, wanting an autograph. There were other airplanes fired up and taxiing behind me, but I couldn't just leave the little boy standing there. I shut down my aircraft and got out and signed his program. We performers are role models and I take it seriously. I want to earn the respect of children. While they were alive, my parents treated me with respect and that's how I want children to feel about me."

Born under the zodiac sign of the crab, Julie lives up to its traits: she is emotional and loving, intuitive and imaginative, a mixture of toughness and softness, shrewd, protective, and sympathetic. In her more than 27,000 flying hours in 65 different types of aircraft, she has impressed tens of thousands of people.

She will never be able to count the many youngsters whose lives she has touched. Yet, she relishes the responses she receives from those who sign her guest book on her website and from the adoring crowds who cluster around her at the end of each of her patriotic and beautiful performances.

As she says, "Sometimes, when I'm signing autographs, little girls will come up and will stand very close beside me. They'll just stare at me, starry-eyed. Those are valuable moments in my life. I couldn't ask for much more than to have inspired young women to push their envelopes and to reach toward greater heights in their own lives. To have shared my sky with others has been my joy; if I've touched young women and helped them to pursue their dreams, I couldn't ask for very much more. I hope their dreams take wing."

**Mentoring other young women
and, after her final flight with Northwest Airlines.
Allan Thomas, "Bravo," shares the Airbus cockpit.**

AFTERWORD: *JUICE PLUS+ SPONSORSHIP*

Julie would like to add a few updates to this now 3rd edition printing in paperback of 2013. Retirement has been a "wonderful thing", although she does miss her co-workers at Northwest Airlines; the other aspects of the job; not so much. The commute to Minneapolis from California is a real "thing of the past!" adds Julie, "I sure don't miss those de-icing lines, and the zero dark thirty get ups either!"

Julie now has accumulated nearly 32,000 hours of flying time and is still very active in the air show business. She has moved her residence, still on Boeing Road at the Cameron Airpark, but 12 houses down. She is in a smaller, very quaint, circular home, but with two hangars! One for the T-28 and one for the T-34!

Julie lost her Minnesota Mom (Gladys) in December of 2010, this left a real hole in her heart; but knows she still flies with her alongside her dad and mom. She also lost one of her very dearest friends, Joe Bellino, to cancer. He had been a part of her ground crew for nearly 10 years and although he lived in Connecticut, they visited often. Joe did so many things to enhance her airplane for uniqueness of smokes and fireworks, etc. in the air show business. He had recently married a wonderful woman, Karen, whom Julie quickly bonded with as well. The three of them were together when Joe passed in May of 2012. He will be sorely missed.

Julie still holds the record of longevity of 19 consecutive years of sponsorship with the same corporation: Mopar Parts of Chrysler. In 2006 that came to a very amicable finish. Julie is very proud to know that no other solo performer has every held a professional relationship with the same corporate sponsor for that length of time. The next four seasons that followed, Julie flew for Chevron Global Aviation. Julie is also proud to still endorse over 22 aviation related products, some for more than 20 years.

Along with her dog Bernie and her bird Ernie, both featured in her book in photos, she also raised a new "family member", Lindy, a Yorkie - Shitzu mix (Shorkie) given to her by her Grand kids. Yes, now two wonderful granddaughters, Emma now 10 (as seen earlier in the book in photos) and Elie now almost 7. Larry, her adopted" (but not on paper) son and wife Nikki moved out to California from Texas, and Larry is now a check airman captain for Polar, now Atlas Air Lines (through mergers!)

The year 2013 marks a new and exciting endeavor for Julie. She and NSA, the makers of Juice Plus+, officially announced their partnership in December 2012. The press release stated: "Juice Plus+, the whole food based nutritional brand, today announced a national partnership with acclaimed air show pilot Julie Clark." NSA and Julie will be taking their campaign, Live Life to the Plus+, to new heights at air shows across the country. The partnership between Clark and Juice Plus+ is ideal as both parties echo the importance of a healthy lifestyle and living life to the fullest. Juice Plus+ went on to say that "Clark truly embodies the Juice Plus+ brand and Lives Life to the Plus. With 40+ years of flight experience and an average of more than 20 air show performances each year, Clark has spent much of her life engaging with and bringing excitement to those around her."

"Having a healthy lifestyle is incredibly important to me" said Julie Clark. "I maintain my health by eating well, taking Juice Plus+ every day and exercising regularly. I've been a customer and a fan of Juice Plus+ since 1999 and am excited to embark on this new journey representing a product that has made a real difference in my life!"

In early 2012, when Julie was seeking a corporate sponsorship, a friend of hers suggested maybe GNC (General Nutrition Center) would be a good fit, since she already had a reputation for staying healthy, eating right and exercising. When Julie thought about the prospects of a sponsorship with GNC she thought, "I'm not a GNC girl, I'm a Juice Plus+ girl."

This "light bulb" moment prompted Julie to call her friends, and Juice Plus+ Representatives, Deana and Bob Christofferson. Deana and Bob were instrumental in helping Julie navigate through the proper channels of getting in front of the key decision makers at NSA. Julie knew that if she had the opportunity to "sell" herself and tell her story, they would also see that she and the Juice Plus+ "family" were a perfect fit. In August of 2012, Julie got her one chance to get in front of NSA's President and Founder, Jay Martin along with 3 of his key leaders. It was at this meeting that Julie, and long-time friend and past president of ICAS (International Council of Air Shows) Gary McMahon, presented Julie's long, stellar career in aviation. Her popularity, longevity; and contribution to air shows, and the fact that air shows reach out to a huge audience of very patriotic, hard working and dedicated Americans and Canadians, made the meeting a success.

Julie is very excited about her new sponsorship and her role as the Live Life to the Plus+ spokesperson for Juice Plus+. She will be traveling across the United States and Canada sharing her story about the advantages and importance of a healthy lifestyle and "Living Life to the Plus+".

NOTHING STOOD IN HER WAY,
Captain Julie Clark

AFFILIATIONS
and
AWARDS

ORGANIZATIONS

Aerobatic Competency Evaluator (ACE)
Aircraft Owners and Pilots Association (AOPA)
Airline Pilots Association (ALPA)-27 years
Alpha Phi Sorority Alumna-Gamma Beta Chapter
California Pilots Association (CPA)
Christian Pilots Association
Commemorative Air Force (CAF)--Life Member
Commemorative Air Force (CAF)-Golden Gate Wing, Northern California
Experimental Aircraft Association (EAA)
F.A.S.T.-Formation and Safety Training - T-34 & T-28 Lead
Friends of Cameron Airpark (FOCA)
International Aerobatic Club (IAC)
International Aerobatic Club-Chapter 69/Phoenix Aerobatic Club (PAC)
International Council of Airshows (ICAS)-Past Director
ISA +21-International Society of Women Airline Pilots-Charter Member
National Aeronautic Association (NAA)
North American Trainer Association (NATA)
The Ninety Nines, International Organization of Women Pilots
Professional Airline Pilots Association (PAPA)
Screen Actors Guild (SAG)
Silver Wings Fraternity-Life Member
The T-34 Association-voted Director - 20 years
Warbirds of America
Warbirds of America-Squadron 11- California
Women in Aviation, International (WAI)

AWARDS

1981:
EAA Convention, Oshkosh: Warbird: Most Improved Warbird (T-34)
Southwest Section, The Ninety-Nines: Woman Pilot of the Year
1982:
Merced West Coast Antique Fly-In: Special Award: Military 1902-1959
Primary Trainer-Monoplane (T-34)

Hollister Fly In: EAA Chapter 62: Special Award
1983:
Named in Outstanding Young Women of America
Merced West Coast Antique Fly-In: First Place Military 1902-1959 Primary Trainer-Monoplane (T-34)
Petaluma Air & Space Bicentennial: Warbirds, Best Judged Aircraft (T-34)
EAA, WI: Warbirds, Special Award, Excellence in Formation Flying
1984:
Captain's Club, International Society of Women Airline Pilots, ISA +21
Merced West Coast Antique Fly-In: First Place Military 1902-1959 Primary Trainer-Monoplane (T-34)
EAA Convention, Oshkosh: Warbirds Division, Ladies Choice
Red Bluff Air Round Up: Best Warbird (T-34)
1985:
Merced West Coast Antique Fly-In: First Place Military 1902-1959 Primary Trainer-Monoplane (T-34)
EAA Chapter 62 Hollister Fly In: Special Award
1986:
Merced West Coast Antique Fly-In: First Place Military 1902-1959 Primary Trainer-Monoplane (T-34)
The Great Livermore Airshow-First Place Special/Custom Aircraft (T-34)
1988:
Albuquerque International Air Show: Children's Choice, Best Performer
Albuquerque International Air Show-Best T-34
GAN Flyer: Readers Choice, Airshow Performer of the Year
GAN Flyer: Readers Choice, Favorite Female Performer
1989:
Who's Who of American Women, 2,000 Notable Women
FAA Certificate of Appreciation for "Outstanding Contribution to Professional Women in Aviation," "Contribution to the Preservation of Military Aircraft," and "Contribution to Women Pioneers in Aviation"
1990:
GAN Flyer, Readers Choice: Favorite Female Performer
1991:

Bill Barber Award for Showmanship: *World Airshow News*
1992:
EAA Warbirds of America: Best T-34 Engine Compartment
GAN Flyer, Readers Choice, Best Air Show Performer, Women's Category
1993:
Inducted, International Forest of Friendship, Atchison, Kansas

1997:
GAN Flyer, Readers Choice, Favorite Overall Performer
GAN Flyer, Readers Choice, Favorite Female Performer
1998:
Art Scholl Memorial Award for Showmanship
1999:
International Council of Air Shows-Best Website, Air Show Performer
2000:
Frances E. Willard Outstanding Alumna Award, Alpha Phi International
Fraternity
Named, Who's Who in Executives & Professionals
2002:
Inducted. Pioneer Hall of Fame, Women in Aviation, International
2003:
Named one of 100 Women Who have Made a Difference in Aviation,
Women in Aviation, International

2011:
Enshrined- International Council of
Air Show Hall of Fame

2012:
Aero Club of Northern California
(NAA) Crystal Eagle Award

Julie is inducted into the
Pioneer Hall of Fame,
Women in Aviation, International
2002

Julie, 13th U.S. Woman
to become a U.S. Airline Pilot,
became a Charter Member of
ISA +21, the
International Society of Women Airline Pilots.
She is seated fourth from the left.

At the Pioneer Hall of Fame Induction,
Women in Aviation, International
2002
with Iris Taggart and Gladys Hood

LAST FORMATION
by Richard A. Emmons, May 1949

I'd like to have a moment, Sir,
Up here so close to You,
To talk about the things I've done
And things I've yet to do.
At times I've left formation,
Peeled off and slipped away,
When 'Move in, close up that gap'
Was the order of the day
I didn't need my compass,
No, not me, I thought I knew.
So I've cursed and made excuses
When my field was overdue.
Each time I've lost my way, Sir,
From my flight with fellow men,
You've found and brought me safely
To formation once again.
And I know that You are watching, Sir,
As I stalk Your halls of air,
For the majesty of Heaven
Is about me everywhere.
And when you form your Squadron, Sir,
And lead these men who fly
On their last and final mission
To Your Air Field in the sky,
I ask that I may be there, Sir,
To make that journey, too.
With throttles to the firewall, Sir,
Let me follow You!

FRIENDS LOST

*Capt. Abe August
*Perry Bales
Bill Barber
Don Beck
Thomas Benton
Rick Brickert
Ken Brockman
Timothy "TJ" Brown
Mike Brundage
Bill and Nancy Champion
*Don Chapman
  Capt. Ernie A. Clark
*Marjorie E. Clark
*Oscar Cleal
*Marilyn Copeland
John Crocker
Vern Dallman
Tom Delashaw "Sharkbait"
Lt. Jim Dobson, USN
*Capt. Lou Dorflinger
Randy Drake
Gordon "Gordy" Drysdale
Eberhart Engle
Keith Evans
* "Tennessee" Ernie Ford
*Joe Foss
Joe Frasca
*Dorothy Hawley
Daniel Heligoin & Montaine
Mallet , The French Connection
*Roger Henderson
Bob Herendeen
Charlie Hillard
Dave Hoover
*Capt. Bill Hughes
Bill Humphreys
Bill Jones
*Fred Jones
Jan Jones

Tom Jones
*Gordon Kibby
*Charles "Kinney" Kinamon
*Leo Loudenslager
Gary Loundagin
Sonny Lovelace
Don Madonna
Rick Massegee
Ray Mabrey
Kirk McKee
*Judy McLane
*Dave Mead
*Fred Meyers
Scott Mills
Tony Olivera
*OD Peterson
Jim Price
Al Pietsch
*Amelia Reid
Frank Sanders
Art Scholl
*Bob Sears
Clancy Speal
*Joan Swisher
*Bobbi Trout
Walt Tubb
Antone Tykody "Pago Jet"
*Dewayne Upton
Stanley Van Vleck
Mike Van Wagenen
Greg Weber
Charlie Wells
*Fay Gillis Wells
James R. Williams
Wes Winters
Steve Wittman
Don Wylie

not due to an aviation accident

214

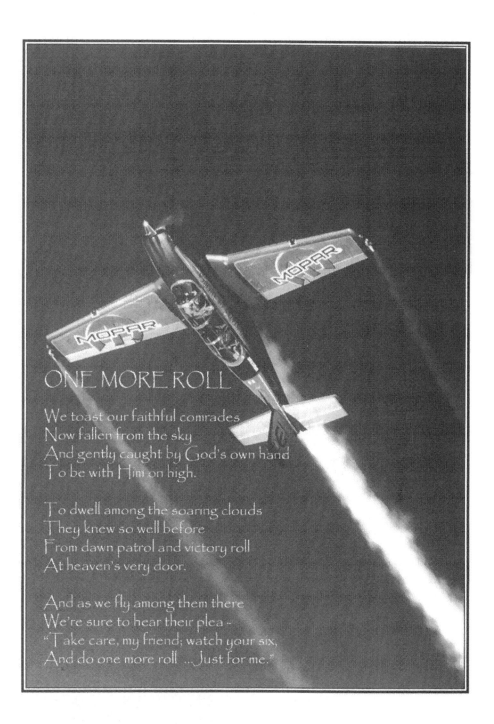

ONE MORE ROLL

We toast our faithful comrades
Now fallen from the sky
And gently caught by God's own hand
To be with Him on high.

To dwell among the soaring clouds
They knew so well before
From dawn patrol and victory roll
At heaven's very door.

And as we fly among them there
We're sure to hear their plea -
"Take care, my friend; watch your six,
And do one more roll ...Just for me."

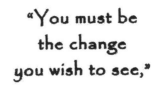

"You must be
the change
you wish to see,"

Mahatma Gandhi
(1869-1948)

FRIENDS CHERISHED
Who Helped Me Along The Way

Penelope Becker
Joe Bellino
Rick Berecz
Bob Bishop
Jerry Blake, (Mopar, Ret.)
J.C. and Gail Brandt
Bob Bowland
Gordon Bowman-Jones
Kay Carter
Chris Ceccarelli
Capt. John Chesley (SFO Helicopter)
Danny Clisham
Duane Cole
Bo Corby
Dave Culp
Sharon DeVos
Bob Donnell
Lou Drendel
Roger "Ramjet" Evans
Sonny Everett
"Daddy" Chuck Fink
Misti Flaspohler
Kurt Flitcroft
Jimmy Franklin
Harriet Fox
Wally Funk
Lefty Gardner
Bob Grant
Judy Grilli
Fred Hale
Wayne Handley
Michelle Harris
Chuck & Jane Holcomb

Gladys Hood "Minnesota Mom"
RA "Bob" Hoover
Vern Jobst
Jerry and Margaret Van Kempen
T.K. King
Larry Littlepage
Capt. Sarge Martin, (NWA Chief Pilot)
Ron McLane "The Fud"
Gary McMahon "Mac"
Duncan Miller
Jim and Marie Moore
Capt. Homer Mouden (Braniff, Ret.)
Charlie, Jim and Jud Nogle
Bob Oliver
Flo Pearson
Ron Pearson "Willy"
Newt Phillips
Capt. J.J. Quinn (Golden West, Ret.)
Gene Ratkowski
General Steve Ritchie
Ed Robinson
Smokey Stover
Iris Taggart
Allan Thomas "Bravo"
Capt. Rick Toscano (NWA Chief Pilot)
General Reg Ursler
Jerry and Judy Van Grunsven
Patty Wagstaff
Chuck Wahl
Jim Williams
Jeana Yeager
Bobby Younkin
Dr. Ralph Glasser
Dean Essenmacher

**Julie's Mopar T-34 boasts a
14-carat gold edition Victor Engine**

BIBLIOGRAPHY

BOOKS:

Coulter, Ann. *SLANDER*, Liberal Lies About the American Right, Three Rivers Press, Crown Publishers, New York, 2002.

Davies, R.E.G. *AIRLINES OF THE UNITED STATES SINCE 1914*, Paladwr Press, Inc., McLean, Virginia, First Published in Great Britain in 1972, Revised Reprinting August 1982, Reprinted 1998.

Encarta 98, Desk Encyclopedia, 1996-1997, Microsoft Corporation

Jones, Geoff. *NORTHWEST AIRLINES*, Plymouth Press, Ian Allan Publishing, Vergennes, VT 05491, 1998.

INTERNET SITES:

http://aviation-safety.net/database
http://military.surfwax.com/files/T-34_Mentor_Plane.html
http://www.airaces.com/fight.html
http://www.agschools.com/
http://www.ashland-city.k12.oh.us/ahs/classes/otis/
http://www.astrology-online.com
http://www.bedeaerosport.com
http://www.centercomp.com/cgi-bin/dc3/gallery?1902
http://www.eaa54.org
http://www.iac.org
http://www.iswap.org
http://www.nwa.com
http://www.personal.psu.edu/users/b/z/bzh102/ist250/sky.htm
http://www.risingup.com/planespecs/info/listBeech.shtml
http://www.usexperiment.org/
http://www.warbirds-eaa.org/cockpit
http://web.nbaa.org/public/news/
http://www.wrhs.org/exhibits/airrace/holman.htm

MAGAZINE ARTICLES:

Beatty, Jenny T., "Emerging Successfully From Mergermania," *AVIATION FOR WOMEN*, Women in Aviation, International, Daytona Beach, Florida, November-December 2000, pages 16-19.

Schloss, Michael, "From the C.O.'s Cockpit," *WARBIRDS*, EAA Warbirds of America, Oshkosh, Wisconsin, December 2000, pages 2-3.

Serling, Robert J. *LOUD AND CLEAR*, The full answer to aviation's vital question: Are the jets really safe? Doubleday & Company, Inc., Garden City, New York, 1969.

Taylor, Michael J.H., Editor. *JANE'S ENCYCLOPEDIA OF AVIATION*, Portland House, New York, 1989. Originally, Jane's Publishing Company Ltd, 1980.

PHOTOGRAPHS:

Unless noted in the margin by the photograph, the images in this book are courtesy of the Julie Clark photograph collection.

INDEX

Curtiss-Wright Airplane Company 80

D

DaimlerChrysler Mopar Parts, 166
DC-8 75
DC-9 45, 145, 202
de Havilland DH-6 111
de Havilland DHC-6 95
Douglas DC-3 31, 67
Douglas DC-4 75
DuPont 166

E

EAA AirVenture 190
EAA AirVenture, 195
Ernie Clark 18, 27
Experiment in International Living 48
Experiment in International Living 49
Experimental Aircraft Association 160
Experimental Aircraft Association (EAA) 120

F

F.27 Friendship 31
Fairchild Industries 31
Federal Aviation Administration 90, 184, 190
Flight 773 35
Flight Guide Publications 166
Fokker Aircraft 31
Forest of Friendship 169
Formation And Safety Team 160
Free Spirit 127
Fresno Air Terminal. 91

G

GAMIjectors 166
Gary Loundagin 134, 135, 136, 138
Gladys Hood 13
Golden West Airlines 94, 97, 98, 106, 109, 112, 113
Golden West Chapter 130
Goleta Airfield 56
Goodrich Weather Mapping Systems 166
Goodyear Aviation Tires 166
Graphic Engine Monitoring System 166

H

Happy Herb 93, 94
Hawkers 62
Hughes Airwest 78, 97, 112, 113, 115, 132, 142, 145, 149

S

T

U

V

W

Made in the USA
Columbia, SC
01 May 2019